Changing Asia

Changing Asia

By Michael Griffiths

Photographs by Fritz Fankhauser

Lion Publishing

Published by Lion Publishing
121 High Street, Berkhamsted, Herts, England

Copyright © 1977 Lion Publishing

First edition 1977

ISBN 0 85648 064 9

Printed in Singapore
by Tien Wah Press Ltd

Contents

One

Change is the Essence of Life

The new apartment blocks in Hong Kong rise among the traditional back-street alleys.

'Change is the essence of life. The moment we cease to change, to be able to adapt, to adjust, to respond effectively to new situations, then we have begun to die.' These are the words of Lee Kuan Yew, Prime Minister of Singapore, quoted in *The Mirror* in 1967.

Change is accelerating rapidly in Asia today. Living inside Asia, travelling frequently within its fascinatingly different countries, it is astonishing to see the changes taking place constantly. Asian change is not a pessimistic 'change and decay'. It is an optimistic, constructive change to better the lives of its changing people.

This book aims to illustrate this fascinating kaleidoscope of change. The coloured fragments arrange and rearrange themselves to make a variety of patterns – but after a while some basic shapes and colours become familiar.

This book is also concerned to ask questions. Where is change taking us? Are changes for the better? It will also look at some of the results of the change, and tackle some of the answers proposed to the question, 'What is the way forward for Asia?'

The visitor to Asia

It used to be the smells of Asia rather than the sights of Asia which first made an impact on the visitor arriving at one of the great seaports of the Far East! Far East of what? The very phrase is the product of an old Europe-centred outlook, and is very definitely out of date today here. But there are still the delicious smells of Chinese food in preparation, of garlic, and pork, sweet and sour, incense and joss-sticks, exotic sandalwood, durian and other fruits. Today, though, it is not so much the scents as the sounds that impress the new arrival, especially the conversation-stopping thunder of jet aircraft coming in to land at every major Asian city.

There are still tourists who come by ship; usually elderly people with the time and money for leisurely and expensive first-class travel. The cheap charter planes spew out the younger visitors in bright caftans and scruffy jeans – though they have to watch their hair-cuts: 'Hippies not admitted' say the signs at the Singapore Causeway; or in the Post Office, 'People with long hair will be served last.' Drop-outs and protesters are features of Western counter-culture which Asia would prefer to do without. Every effort is made to exclude the drug culture, every bit as unwelcome as opium was in China. Even the innocent 'Puff the Magic Dragon' is banned from Singapore record shops as a cannabis song.

The harbours of Singapore and Hong Kong are as crowded as ever (though not with passenger shipping), and probably as smelly, for Hong Kong's tides dispose of thousands of tons of sewage daily. The ever-climbing buildings seem to be competing with the jumbo jets for air-space. Hong Kong is currently four storeys ahead of Singapore whose newest tallest building is the Overseas Chinese Banking Centre, 66oft and fifty-two storeys high. The deafening roar of aircraft thundering down over these buildings remains the dominant impression. In the crowded airport lounges, sound is again dominant, with the strident tones of native Cantonese almost blotted out by the polite polysyllables of the Japanese tourists.

Tourists are everywhere with their Japanese cameras and cassette-players, visiting the relics of early European adventures: the Forts of Malacca and Macassar, the Raffles Gardens in Bogor, West Java, and many other legacies of the colonial period. They gaze at Portuguese buildings in Macao and Malacca, enjoy French bread in Laos, wrinkle their noses at the Dutch canals in Djakarta (the sense of smell still re-asserts itself there!), relish the Spanish guitars and dress in the Philippines and admire Japanese architecture and railways in Taiwan (a reminder that not all colonial powers were European).

Language is the most persistent legacy of colonialism. University education in Cambodia was still in French until 1975, and many of the Chinese and Indonesians in Java still speak Dutch by preference.

Early traders went in search of exotic spices to enliven the European housewife's salted meat. Today merchant shipping carries Asian produce to markets all over the world.

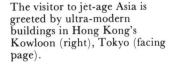

The visitor to jet-age Asia is greeted by ultra-modern buildings in Hong Kong's Kowloon (right), Tokyo (facing page).

The villagers of Northern
Thailand still wear their
attractive tribal dress: this woman
(left) is from the Yao tribe.
Time-honoured washday rituals
in Taiwan (right) are adapted to
the new technology!

A dancer in Bangkok (left)
performs now for the tourists, not
for religious rites. Pert young lady
(right) from Lawas, Sarawak,
represents the new generation,
complete with 'shock' hat . . .

An Akha tribal woman in her
kitchen in mountainous North
Thailand wears the distinctive
dress of her tribe.

The mountains and paddy-fields
of Taiwan (following page), with
buffalo-drawn plough, represent
the beauty and centuries-old
traditions of rural Asia which are
being changed so rapidly today.

Transport in fast-moving Asia typifies the changing life-styles. The two young ladies paddling their sampan, the men with the motorized equivalents, and the slow-moving Yao ox-cart, are all from Thailand. The crowded motor-cycle and splendidly baroque decoration of the bus were seen in the Philippines. Tokyo's subway is packed at rush-hour time, as tired commuters return to their high-rise apartments and suburban homes.

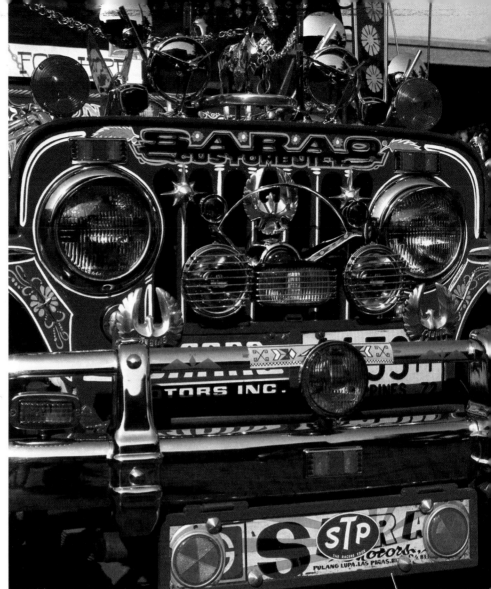

Traditional and modern high-rise: a contrast in styles. A pagoda in the mountain area of Taiwan (above) and apartment blocks in Hong Kong (left). Hong Kong's massive government building programme is vital to keep up with the demand for apartments. Space allocation per person has now increased: even so, the pressures on family life are enormous. Many escape from the tower blocks into the stress of student or business life, or crowd the busy shopping areas.

Older people in Taiwan and Korea can still speak Japanese, although they prefer not to do so. English is widely spoken and taught in schools all over Asia, as well as being the first language of many in Singapore and the Philippines. All languages show plenty of borrowing from others: whether 'sekolah', 'teksi', 'basu', 'kelabu' in Malay or those barely recognizable Japanese words derived from the German 'arbeit', the French 'avec' or 'vacance', and innumerable English words such as 'sebiro' (Saville Row) for a man's jacket, and ungainly abbreviations such as 'suto' for strike, 'masukomu' for mass communication and 'ensto' for engine-stop!

In the Philippines, near the Taal Volcano, there is one of the oldest Roman Catholic churches in Asia. In Djakarta, you will discover the oldest Dutch Protestant church building in Asia, formerly a Portuguese Catholic church until it experienced conversion by decree of the Dutch East India Company.

Is a new man emerging?

But Asia's past is rooted more in Asia itself than in imports from the West. Evidence of the reflective Asian imagination can be seen everywhere in traditional religion. Indian influence is implied by the very names of former Indo-China and Indonesia. In Java, there is the magnificent Buddhist Temple of Borobadur, while Bali is still predominantly Hindu. Near Jogjakarta, tourists may watch evening performances of ancient Hindu epic dances in the Wayang plays performed in the open air with the beautiful ruins of the Prabanan as a moonlit backcloth. In Hirosaki, northern Japan, you may walk beneath the cascading cherry blossom near the castle, with snow-clad Mount Iwaki in the distance, and visit the sixty-six Zen temples collected together in two streets.

Alongside are the new religions of Asia. In just a few years after the war, Japan invented more than one hundred new ones, registered with the Ministry of Education for tax exemption purposes. Among them is the militant Sookagakkai with its political arm the Clean Government Party. In Korea, there is the Unity Church of Mr Moon, using up-to-date public relations methods to spread his doctrine. In the Philippines, visitors admire the sugar-icing architecture of the Manalo sect church buildings.

The old religion of Mammon, the worship of money and capitalistic materialism, is to be found alongside the worship of the progress of the state, the new religion of Marx, Lenin and Mao. Communism is vigorously suppressed in some countries, insurgent in the jungles of others, and accepted as the ruling ideology in Laos, Cambodia, Vietnam, North Korea and supremely in mainland China. In Hong Kong, apart from those who come in openly by ship and jumbo jet, there are always those dissenters from Maoism who swim in secretly and perilously across Cold Bay from the mainland.

The old and the new are found together as inseparably as sweet and sour. In Hong Kong there are hydrofoils and junks, and

Workers at a Taiwan temple.

A pattern of sampans, West Malaysia.

television antennae sprout on the sampans of the boat people. In Thailand, elephants and bulldozers work side by side, making new roads. You can cross the mighty Mekong River by helicopter, or by dug-out canoe. In Japan, there are electrically heated toilet-seats in some homes, but still the traditional septic pits in many others.

The governments offer new ideals: in Singapore the 'rugged society' is 'clean, green and gracious' (encouraged by a little material inducement in the form of harsh fines for litter-bugs); the 'new Filipino' is a positive consequence of Martial Law; and a Tokyo government White Paper proposes 'the image of the Japanese to be expected'.

But there are always dissenters: the dissidents in the jungles of Malaysia or the followers of the Triple Negatives in Japan (no interest, no feeling, no enthusiasm). New religions replace the obsolete. Fresh governments replace the old. People who once lived in horizontal rows now dwell in vertical piles. In Japan, you wade out from the shore not through skeins of seaweed (most of which has been eaten), but through the debris of inedible plastic bags and indestructible bottles. Is there any modern Aladdin who can give us new lamps for old? Can you find a genie in a plastic bottle?

Can we get new man for old?

Does Asia have answers for the alienated man of technocratic society?

A modern Japanese short story points the problem. Evening rush-hour trains disgorge their commuters – the men, with dark hair and

This street in Taiwan is typical of Asian city life, the streets often jammed with cars and buses.

horn-rimmed glasses, in dark business-suits carry almost identical briefcases. Along the road to the Danchi, a row of identical high-rise apartments, each block only distinguishable from its neighbour by a different serial number. One of the commuters selects one of a number of identical staircases, climbs past a number of identical floors and selects rather carelessly one of a number of identical doors. Upon entering, he notices immediately that something is wrong.

His wife has exchanged the position of the settee and one of the matching armchairs on opposite sides of the television set. A few new books have suddenly appeared on the shelves, and the pictures on the walls have been changed. Someone comes in from the kitchen wearing the familiar off-the-peg dress. His wife appears to have done something to her hair. An alarmed stare convinces him that she has changed her

Factory workers in Taiwan assemble electronic equipment and make goods for export all over the world, then cycle back to their hostel accommodation (see too pictures on pages 28, 34, 75).

face as well. Horrors! It is not his wife at all! He has made a mistake and climbed one floor too many. He makes his embarrassed apologies and hurries back downstairs and, descending, passes another man with identical dark hair, horn-rimmed glasses, dark business-suit and identical briefcase.

Arriving in his own flat, he begins to analyse his experience. All the rooms in the block are the same size and shape. They all have a television set in the corner. They buy their furniture from the same multiple stores. The shelves contain almost entirely identical books, for all have been through the same stereotypéd educational system. They all use the same detergents and deodorants, for all watch the same television commercials. The other wife was remarkably like his own and the other husband was remarkably like himself. We are all like a lot of ants in a vast hygienic human ant-heap! We are all being programmed by education, by the media, we are all becoming more and more alike!

A week later, as he travels in the train, he has a pleasing sense of being different from common commuters. Of all the men in this rush-hour train, he alone is carrying dynamite and detonators in his briefcase. But as he contorts himself to hang from the strap, to hold the briefcase under his arm and read the evening paper, his eye is caught by a significant paragraph. There is a photograph of someone looking remarkably like himself, living in the next block of flats. He has killed himself with an explosive device carried in his briefcase . . .

Theodore Roszak, in *The Making of a Counter-Culture*, sees nothing at the end of the technocratic road but, 'Two sad tramps forever waiting under that wilted tree for their lives to begin, except that I think the

Are the new city-scapes of Asia making people no more than machines in boxes, programmed to a stereotyped existence, without freedom, without individuality?

tree isn't going to be real, but a plastic counterfeit. In fact, even the tramps may turn out to be automatons . . . Of course, there will be great programmed grins on their faces.'

How can a man find his identity in a society becoming increasingly overcrowded, where everyone is being manipulated and programmed by the mass media to become more and more alike?

What are the factors that are making man change and where are they taking him?

Two

What is Changing Asia?

The forces for change are dramatically highlighted in Phnom Penh: war, commerce, urbanization, new blocks rising behind traditional thatched houses.

The Japanese were once pictured as leisurely, kimono-clad figures moving gracefully under the cherry blossoms, over ornamental bridges with a backcloth of snowcapped Mount Fuji. Now perhaps their popular image is that of highly successful, golf-playing industrialists.

The allegedly 'characteristic' aspects of different cultures are rapidly disappearing. We regret the passing of old ways of life, and we are not comforted by the plastic imitations cooked up by the tourist industry who offer us a commercialized Ainu village in Hokkaido and Thai dancing in Bangkok hotels. We fear that the real thing has been lost for ever. Yet we cannot turn the clock back: change seems inevitable. The old life is only preserved for us in books, ancient Japanese prints, old films and fading photographs.

The rate of change has accelerated in this century as a result of the invention of the automobile and aeroplane, the introduction of the new political ideas, the ideal of universal education, the quest for social justice, and above all by being more closely linked together than ever before in the 'global village'. Life in the old world was described by Macbeth as 'a tale told by an idiot'.

Is life any better when told by a 'global village' idiot?

What then are the factors accelerating change in Asia today?

Trade and commerce

The great voyages of exploration of previously unknown countries were made by merchants wanting to buy and sell and make a profit. It was Chinese merchants who developed the 'south-pointing fish', originally an astrological divining-board with 'a south-pointing spoon', as a navigational aid: they were six hundred years ahead of Europe in using the magnetic compass. Amusingly, the basic motive behind the intrepid European explorers was nothing more exciting than food! The European winter diet was very dull and the spices of the 'Indies' were in great demand to make their diet more tasty during the dark cold months.

Merchants wanting to buy silk, tea and other commodities from China had to offer something which the Chinese wanted in exchange.

The centuries-old pattern of Asian market trading seen here in Bangkok remains unchanged, apart from the scales!

Such cargo must not weigh too much. It is a sad fact that during Queen Victoria's Sixty Glorious Years on average a ton of opium left India for China every two hours. The weight factor is still significant, for tribesmen in North Thailand continue to grow the opium poppy today. There is nothing else so easily transported which is worth so much money. Other money crops such as vegetables and fruit are much heavier to transport where there are no roads, and fruit goes bad before you can sell it. It was this vile opium trade which wrecked the relationships between China and the Western nations and led to terrible wars. Political tensions in the world today can be traced back to this basic economic cause.

The picking of tea and tapping of rubber in Malaya required cheap labour, and as Malays were disinclined to supply it, large numbers of Tamil labourers were brought from India. When Raffles decided to found the city of Singapore on a small muddy island off the Malay Peninsula in 1819, its total population was ninety Malays living by

The colourful romance of the East, the money to be made from jewels and spices, was Asia's original appeal to western merchants. The traditional splendour is preserved in the finery of this Taiwanese tribal girl.

piracy on vessels passing through the straits of Malacca. Within a few months of Raffles' arrival, however, there were several thousand Chinese immigrants there beginning to make their fortunes by buying and selling. The cities of South-East Asia grew not˙ because of industrialization and people flocking in from the surrounding country areas, but by population overflow from China. Fortune hunters came from the coastal provinces of China to make money, a characteristic that remains to this day.

The university courses most favoured by men in Singapore and Malaysia are still economics, business administration and commerce. Western medicine is also popular, because it is a lucrative skill that can be exercized elsewhere, if political pressures make it expedient to move. The tin industry in Malaya was exploited largely by Chinese hard work. Throughout the region there is still tension between the industrious Chinese who make money (and deserve to do so), and the more leisurely indigenous peoples of the region, who suddenly discover that much of their nation's wealth is owned by hardworking immigrants. This is true in Malaysia, Indonesia, Thailand and the Philippines and explains the existence of racial tension, frightening violence and political discrimination. Trade and the profit motive have been significant influences in shaping Asian societies.

All over East Asia today there are flashing neon signs advertising the great Japanese brand names – Honda, Toshiba, Akai, Sony, Mazda, Toyota, National: cameras, cars, motorbikes, cassette recorders, stereoplayers and hifi radios. Japanese business firms are helping to develop new industrial complexes such as Jurong in Singapore, Kiaoshung in Taiwan. In some Asian countries today, a growing reaction against Japanese industrial expansion is noticeable. As trade increases, the way of life changes again; the roads become congested and overcrowded, new roads have to be built, often by foreign firms. Country people begin to find it more lucrative to work for these firms than to work on their farms. They earn money which enables them to buy a motorbike or a car and provides the possibility of commuting to work in the town, or selling up and moving to the big city. So the cities grow, the price of land rises, people move into high-rise housing developments away from the scattered kampongs, traffic becomes still more congested and pollution increases.

Life in the city

In Asia, the great cities preceded industrialization by many years. Edo had a population of one million people in the year 1800 when London was a small place of six hundred thousand. What happened to Edo? Today, it is called Tokyo. The other great South-East Asian cities such as Saigon, Singapore, Hong Kong, Batavia (Djakarta) and Manila grew more as centres of Western colonial administration, providing necessary services and opportunity for entrepreneurs, than as a result of industrialization.

Urbanization statistics are notoriously deceptive. You may say that

An opium user, and the opium poppy being cultivated (left) – illustrating not only present-day drug problems but the opium wars and political trafficking in opium during the last century, continued in the drug rackets of today.

The floating market at Bangkok (left); fishing, and fish laid out to dry, in Thailand (right).

The shift of population to the cities has brought its own problems. The rapid growth of Djakarta, Indonesia, to a city of 5 million people has put enormous strain on services such as power and water supply. The canals, a legacy of Dutch colonial rule, are all too easily used for the disposal of rubbish and as latrines.

The small port of Masan, Korea, illustrates the growth of town to city with the expansion of trade.

In Taiwan, girls are recruited for the factories of Kaosiung where applied technology and a massive labour force turn out goods cheaply to capture world markets.

Businesses in Hong Kong's commercial areas (opposite page) compete for tourists' duty-free purchases, as well as international trade.

The drift to the cities: lights
gleam as the sun sets behind
Masan, Korea; snow over the
northern Japanese city of
Sapporo; Hong Kong straddling
its famous harbour – the
commercial centre of Hong Kong
island below, Kowloon across the
bay. A play area in Singapore
(right) provides an outlet for the
energies of families in the
high-rise flats.

Growing up in Asia: children of Sarawak; and a Karen tribal woman.

80 per cent of Asians live in villages. You may also say that 63 per cent of Asians live in cities! The difference in these statistics depends upon the size of town which you arbitrarily decide to call a city. Thus the following figures give a truer picture:

20% of Asians live in communities larger than 20,000
43% of Asians live in communities between 10,000 and 20,000
37% of Asians live in communities smaller than 10,000

Something of the tremendous drift from more scattered rural populations to the larger towns and cities can be seen from the following figures:

1. Asian Population

1920 = 1023 million
1960 = 1652 million
1980 = 2404 million (estimated)

Total population percentage increase in 40 years: 61%
Total population percentage increase in 20 years: $45\frac{1}{2}$%

2. Urban Population (20,000 plus)

1920 = 66 million
1960 = 276 million
1980 = 536 million (estimated)

Urban population percentage increase in 40 years: 318%
Urban population percentage increase in 20 years: 95%

3. Primate Cities (over 500,000 plus)

Primate city population (increase from 1920 to 1960 only): 640%

These figures show very clearly that the larger the city the more rapid its growth.

In Japan in the fifteen years after the Pacific War, the number of Japanese involved in agriculture dropped from 40 per cent to 11 per cent. Wherever this tremendous population drift to the cities takes place, it brings about further inevitable changes in social structure. In the country farming area, the father was not only the head of the family, but also the head of the family farming business, and the respected authority on the traditional ways of doing things. Frequently the extended family, with three or four generations living under the ancestral roof, attained considerable size.

In *Chinese Looking-Glass* Dennis Bloodworth describes how his wife grew up within a vast, walled enclosure in China where 'lived, ate and slept four generations of the Liang family with their wives, their concubines, their children and their numerous servants – about eight hundred souls in all'. She herself was the 'eighth child of the seventeenth son of the patriarch'.

The family was closely knit and mutually interdependent with the

Kaosiung factory girls are housed in hostels, far from home and family life.

Students in Manila: Pressures on students can be intense, not helped by over-crowded homes where study is difficult.

framework of labour on the land. When such a family moves to the city, the children begin to work for other employers and father stops being their employer. Soon children know more about living in the city than their father does. He is no longer the expert and begins to lose his authority; the family structure begins to change and young people begin to move out from their ancestral home. They are now financially independent and set up their small, nuclear-family homes. The wallspace formerly occupied by the altar for ancestral worship is now occupied by a television set with several colour channels. The 'have-nots' flood from the villages to the growing cities, expecting to become the 'haves'. They find that the opportunity for 'going up in the world' is not for everyone and become the discontented 'drop-outs' of the new slums. If they are not manipulated into acceptance of their role by the media, they are likely to be manipulated into following the next plausible political revolutionary who can win them over.

Unless there is deliberate governmental control, the wealthy city immigrants will continue to grow richer, while the country peasants remain as they always have been. Adventurous people with initiative and drive move out to the cities and start to make money, at the expense of the poorer and less adventurous rural population. Such a situation is potentially explosive and likely to lead to a succession of revolutions so that responsible governments cannot necessarily be 'free-for-all' democracies, but must exercise some control of human greed and selfishness to ensure that the riches and profits are enjoyed not only by a fortunate few, but by the population as a whole.

The plight of young people living in such a changing society is well described by A. A. Lamer in the WSCF Magazine: 'Set adrift in a culture which could give him no community to belong to, he is left hanging, floating aimlessly in space: his feet far beyond the gravitational pull of the society into which he was born, the earth which his forefathers had trod so firmly; his hand unable to grasp any of the stars of his new ambitions and desires in the blue but void skies of the new learning.'

Technology goes hand-in-hand with urbanization. But technology too is nothing new. The Chinese have always been essentially practical and pragmatic people. They were making wheelbarrows a thousand years before they appeared in Europe. They produced the first seismograph for recording earthquakes in AD 132. Three centuries before the English archers took the field at Agincourt, the Chinese were using gunpowder grenades enclosed in bamboo casing, and by Shakespeare's time they had batteries of rocket-launchers mounted on barrows. The Chinese had iron-chain suspension bridges a thousand years before Europe's first. The Chinese were drilling for natural gas before Christ was born. The Koreans invented movable type three hundred years before Gutenberg.

Even if such skills are not new, the pace of the growth of technology has accelerated enormously. Today it is both a force for change and a result of change in Asian society. Japan today is the world's greatest producer of ships; it ranks third in the production of steel and is rapidly capturing world markets with motorcars and motorbikes, as well as with cameras and electronic equipment. Within Japan there are flourishing industries for the production of sports equipment for skiers, golfers and mountaineers. Tourism is a formidable industry and giant hotels continue to go up in all the great Asian cities. Building technology is altering the way in which people live.

The high-rise apartment complexes in Hong Kong and Singapore

The pressure on space in Kowloon, Hong Kong, pushes buildings skywards and bus transport overhead – with talk of multi-level planning for the city of the future.

Young people sit and talk as the lights come up over the harbour, Manila.

are especially striking. In warmer climates, they may not isolate their occupants to the same extent as they do in Europe and America, but nonetheless they bring in a host of new problems. With laundry poles on the sunny side and television aerials on the other side, there is a lack of space for growing vegetables or flowers. The lack of privacy for study or courtship means that young people crowd into the parks after dark for privacy. The streets of Seoul, Korea, in the warmer evenings are filled with aimless young people looking for excitement and meaning in life.

But how can we escape the drab monotony of life in a technocratic society?

War

War changes society more quickly and traumatically than any other factor. For the first half of the twentieth century Japan was virtually under the control of militaristic thinking. There was the resounding defeat of Russia at the hands of the Japanese Navy, the annexation of Manchuria and of Korea, the invasion of China and finally the fantastic whirlwind attack which followed Pearl Harbour, when within the space of a few weeks Japan occupied most of South-East Asia and was advancing into India in the west and threatening both Alaska to the north and Australia to the south.

Older people in nearly every East Asian country have memories of Japanese occupation. For the Japanese, to surrender meant dishonour, and until the closing stages of the war only one prisoner was taken for every thousand dead. The end of the war meant not only the destruction of the Japanese military empire, but also that Japan itself was left ravaged and desolate. It was not only that the cities of Nagasaki and Hiroshima had been devastated by the first atomic bomb attacks. The capital city of Tokyo itself had been razed to the ground by systematic incendiary attack from low-flying American bombers. There was so little food available that many Japanese were too weak to work. The effect of this terrible experience upon the older generation who went through this defeat was no less significant than the intense hatred of war which it engendered in the younger generation..

War has been the predominant influence in Vietnam for very many years. For more than a generation the effort and endeavour of the country has gone into fighting wars rather than into economic development. Wasteful deaths of young Vietnamese men reduced the possibility of marriage for a whole generation of young women. War leaves a host of orphans and widows to be cared for and supported. Money is spent on purchasing weapons to kill people rather than on prospering men's lives.

War drives thousands of people from their homes. Vietnam, Laos and Cambodia have very large refugee problems. The population of the city of Phnom Penh increased from half a million to two million people: three out of every four were refugees. When the war ended, these people were all driven out into the countryside by force. There are still groups of Cambodian and Vietnamese refugees scattered around the world. There are camps in Thailand, in Sarawak and on an island off Singapore, as well as in France and the United States. The suffering of people who have lost their homes and members of their families, who have left their businesses behind them and must now endeavour to eke out an existence on the charity of others is appalling. International relief organizations do their best to help. National governments are not keen that the refugees should be made too comfortable and would rather encourage them to return to the countries from which they have come.

Certainly the older colonial powers, the French and the Dutch, like the Spanish and the Portuguese before them, have been driven out. The presence of American forces, while doubtless serving to stem for a time the advance of Communism, has been an unhelpful factor in many ways economically, for it has provided a livelihood to a large number of racketeers, profiteers, bar hostesses and the like. The identification of the United States with the 'Christian' West has been unfortunate to say the least. It is not surprising if Asians seeing the behaviour of American servicemen in the parasitic areas surrounding their bases should decide that if this was 'Christianity', they did not particularly want it. The general attitude of racial superiority assumed by such military forces was scarcely calculated to endear them to the Asian people who came into contact with them. If opium was once the great hindrance to the spread of Christianity in China, the Vietnam War has probably been the great hindrance to the spread of Christianity in East Asia for the past quarter-century.

Communism

Communism has been a major factor for change: not only in those countries which now have Communist governments, but also in those which so far have rejected it. In Malaysia, combating 'the emergency'

Machine-guns and road-blocks have become all too familiar in parts of Asia torn by war.

resulted in scattered Chinese settlers being gathered together into the 'New Villages'. In Indonesia, in the days following the attempted coup, hundreds of thousands of people were executed and the rivers of Java filled with drifting headless corpses for days. Even today there are said to be many thousands of people held in detention camps.

On the northern borders of Thailand, Communist insurgency meant that many Meo tribal people fled down to the plains and were resettled in refugee villages. At the time when eastern Laos was first occupied by Communist forces, the areas remaining around the towns on the Mekong River were full of refugee tribespeople. In Japan and the Philippines (before Martial Law) Communist-inspired demonstrating students threw Molotov cocktails and pill-box bombs at the police. The Huks were in open rebellion in the central provinces of Luzon. Security forces have been harrassed throughout Thailand and parts of Malaysia.

This cultural change is not merely accidental. Rather the whole purpose of Communist ideology is to bring about the overthrow of existing governments, by violence if necessary. Whole populations have been terrorized, required to pay ransom and protection money in attempts to bring about the overthrow of national governments. While some regimes have undeniably been self-interested and riddled with graft and corruption, others have been honest governments seeking the maximum benefit of the greatest possible number of their countrymen. Yet human life is threatened by violence from subversive forces on the one hand and from civil authorities struggling to maintain order on the other:

One of the first uses of barbed wire was beneficial – enabling mid-west US settlers to keep the herds of cattle off their land and homes. Now it is more often seen as the symbol of violence and war, of man's inhumanity to man.

individuals have agonizing choices to make for themselves and their families.

Among university students, the writings of Marx and Mao have been formative in their thinking, whether acceptable to the authorities or not. Universities have been thrown into turmoil with the organization of activist cells, indoctrination and demonstrations. University students are nearly always idealistic and are particularly nauseated by adult hypocrisy and corruption. Marxism and Maoism have seemed the best possible hope of change and improvement available. They have seldom seen any alternatives.

Philippino students distributed a manifesto called 'Is Violence the Way?' in which they spoke out strongly against what they called 'the brutal and violent over-reaction of the police'. They then went on to say, 'We must coldly scrutinize any premature or hasty suggestion that an armed revolution is necessary, imminent, and/or inevitable. Revolution is an illusive and dubious instrument of change. There is no guarantee that the system that would arise out of the bloodied warpath of class struggle would be any better than the corrupt and perverted structure it is seeking to replace.'

That particular time of turmoil in the Philippines produced some creative thinking and writing about their problems and the solutions to them. One of their leaders wrote: 'The Marxist analysis of the source of corruption is true enough to be interesting, but, like every heresy, it is false when taken as the whole truth. Have they verified that human corruptness is primarily economic? What real evidence is there that people become unselfish when their economic needs are met? Marxism is too simplistic and too optimistic about human nature.'

Thus, while it is true that both Marxism and Maoism have been major factors in cultural change, they have also provoked not merely a reactionary antithesis but also a resultant synthesis which may in the long run be more productive. Certainly it cannot be verified that human corruptness is primarily economic. There is no evidence that in European and North American communities, where people's economic needs are met, the people have consequently become unselfish. Here is another problem of the human heart for which changing Asia is desperately seeking a solution.

Government policy

Government policy is properly a major factor in the changes taking place in Asia today. Because ethnic minorities such as immigrants and tribal communities are particularly susceptible to subversion, it naturally becomes government policy to integrate them into the nation by educating them in the majority language. Whereas many aboriginal tribes had been neglected as second-class citizens, more recently in the Philippines, Thailand and Malaysia, government help has been given to mountain tribes in the hope of integrating them and giving them a sense of loyalty to their country.

Sometimes official pressure has also been exerted to persuade people

Opposite page: A Christian girl of the Akha tribe of Northern Thailand winnowing grain.

to embrace the predominant religious convictions of the country: Buddhism in Thailand, Islam in Malaysia, and Roman Catholicism in the Philippines. It is understandable that nations will encourage the integration of minorities, even though it may mean the loss of some traditional aspects of indigenous culture. But when it comes to changing beliefs, there are problems.

In Indonesia, the five points of the Constitution (Pantya Sila) give first place to 'worship of the one God', using an ambiguous word which may refer to Allah or to the Lord of the Christians or even to the monistic totality of the Hindus. Indonesia is thus a monotheistic country, and there is strong social pressure towards acceptance of the majority religions and away from animism. Many former animists have been changing either to Islam or to Christianity. Indeed, if they enjoy eating pork the choice is a simple one, and they embrace Christianity! Islam normally forbids the eating of pork, although more recently jungle people have been allowed a dispensation to continue to use pork and wild boar as a major source of protein, in order that this might not hinder their religious conversion.

In mainland China the Constitution allows 'freedom to believe in religion, freedom not to believe in religion and freedom to propagate atheism'. Freedom to propagate religion is the significant omission. Even offering somebody a New Testament could be interpreted as interfering with that individual's 'freedom not to believe in religion'. So government policy influences the religious belief or unbelief of its citizens. True religious freedom demands not only freedom to propagate but also the basic right of all men to change their religion if they so desire. It is this kind of freedom which is still denied to many people in Asia today.

Many responsible governments are deeply concerned about family planning and birth control. In the Philippines, 47 per cent of the population is under fifteen years of age and the government has done its best to introduce and encourage family planning, in spite of opposition from the Roman Catholic church. Posters in Singapore remind us that 'small families have more things' and that 'two children are enough even if both are girls'! A recurring problem is that while better-educated wealthier families understand the need for population control and accept government policy, poorer illiterate people go on having large families because every additional child is another wage-earner for the family. Because this tends to 'breed out the brains' it has been partially compensated for by legislation. Maternity leave with pay is allowed only for the first two children, and hospital expenses are made prohibitively high after the second child.

In Japan there is social pressure exerted by neighbourhood mothers to terminate a third or fourth pregnancy. In Indonesia, birth control posters show the misery of the large family compared with the small, happy family with only two or three children. It is nonetheless questionable whether the population as a whole has got the message: to simpler people 'family planning' means to plan for a baby a year! Malthus was the man who first drew the world's attention to the

Harvesting in the rice-fields of
Toraja, Sulawesi, Indonesia.

Home of the Hanunoo tribesmen
in the Philippines.

Akha people of Northern Thailand make up decorations for their elaborate traditional head-dresses (above). Women return (right) from the market at Ranau in Sabah, East Malaysia.

Many in the West are looking for more communal styles of living in reaction to soulless apartment blocks and the lostness of city life. In the traditional longhouses of Sarawak (left), family and community life are successfully integrated.

Inside a longhouse: each family has its own quarters opening off a communal hallway.

A way out of a very human dilemma: a childless Yao couple visit the Akha tribe to buy a child. Traditional customs must stand the pressures of modern life, answer the challenge – or be lost, as they so often are, in the move to the cities.

Confrontation between old and new at Aberdeen, Hong Kong. The junks and sampans with their floating population have TV aerials, and are overlooked by surrounding tower blocks. Radio and television influence and mould different peoples from many backgrounds into the new way of life.

Japanese children in their secondary school uniforms; and a Japanese child on her way to school through the snow in Sapporo.

Traffic halts at Japan's pedestrian crossings', allowing the crowds across to the subway station before the lights change.

Violence and war have torn the soul out of many communities, leaving families decimated, the economy ruined and thousands homeless. This picture was taken at Phnom Penh just after a rocket attack.

Exploitation of the workers or over-greedy capitalism can provide a ready audience for Communist ideas.

In the rural area of Manorom, Thailand, life continues as it has for centuries past – fishing, fetching water, pausing to pass the time of day as the sun sinks toward the horizon.

danger of over-population and consequent food shortage through a famous essay on population written in the nineteenth century: small wonder that overcrowded Java was once known as 'the despair of Malthus'! Government policy affects the number of children in a family. In earlier days of high infant mortality, families might commonly have five, six or seven surviving children. Today, it is becoming commonplace in several Asian countries for people to have no more than two or three children.

In the Philippines, the skilful use of television slogans has sought to encourage the development of 'the new Filipino'. In Singapore, people have learnt 'to keep Singapore clean' by the negative inducement of heavy fines on people leaving litter or allowing mosquitoes to breed. In Japan, a government White Paper pictured 'the ideal Japanese to be expected' – though failed to explain how it might be attained. Like most humanist (and some religious) moralities it urges people to live considerately and unselfishly, without telling them how to do it – like the man who placed an ostrich egg in front of a bantam hen and commanded, 'Keep your eyes on this and do your best'!

It will be seen that government policy is a major factor for social change throughout Asia. This is good and useful where it can be seen that changes need to be made for the benefit of society as a whole. Nonetheless, to have to decide on these changes is a heavy responsibility for the politician, who knows only too well that he is anything but omniscient. Every change leads to further, sometimes unexpected, side-effects, producing yet more change.

A further factor for change, however, comes from governments quite outside Asia. It has become fashionable for wealthier governments in 'developed' countries to offer financial aid to 'developing' countries, with or without strings attached. Sometimes this has been done to prop up a regime considered democratic and which might well collapse without such financial encouragement to maintain its weak ideological convictions. Elsewhere aid has been more altruistic, although sometimes those responsible for supervision have torn their hair in efforts to prevent misappropriation by greedy officials eager to line their own nests or enhance their own reputation.

Much help has been given by generous governments to assist developing countries with educational programmes, particularly at university level. In Indonesia, Russia has trained technicians while the Dutch, German and British governments have given grants to help equip some scientific departments in universities. The Singapore and German governments have established a joint Television Training Centre to train people from several South-East Asian countries in television production. Many countries also offer scholarships in their own universities for training Asians, and thus more people gain a wider view of the world.

Education

The significant effects of increased literacy in exposing whole populations to new and revolutionary ideas cannot be overestimated. Once people

Books on a night-market bookstall. Education in general and reading in particular have opened up whole new areas of life and experience to ordinary people.

have learnt to read, then only the very strictest censorship will prevent them having access to unpopular opinions. Something of the scale of this change will be understood, when we realize that at the end of the Pacific War in 1945, after three centuries of Dutch rule, only 11 per cent of Indonesians were literate: but twenty years later, in 1965, as many as 65 per cent of Indonesians were literate. Fifty million more people could read Indonesian.

In post-war South-East Asia, freed from direct colonialist influences, there was a tremendous development of a secular system of state education modelled upon Western systems. The new target was universal education and an immense expansion began.

The numbers in secondary education between 1950 and 1960 doubled in Indonesia, tripled in Thailand, increased by five times in South Vietnam, by six times in Malaya and by almost ten times in Cambodia.

Large numbers of teachers were trained in a hurry, the standards of the secondary schools began to fall, and inevitably a lower standard of entry was accepted for the universities. Many children dropped out along the way for a variety of reasons: for every thousand children entering primary school in Malaya, only fifty completed secondary education; in Thailand only twenty-five; in Indonesia only twenty; in Cambodia only nine.

For every thousand boys entering primary school in Thailand in 1950, only four remained in school to matriculate in 1962 and probably two of these graduated from the university in 1965 or 1966.

The result of this 'educational inflation' is that the necessity of a 'modern education' in order to obtain salaried work is increasingly emphasized. At first, secondary education is essential; then as jobs fill up, a university degree is needed. Pressure mounts to expand secondary schools (whether there are teachers or not), and standards fall; then there is pressure to reduce the level of entrance to the university, which is now too hard for the less well-prepared secondary pupil. In order to win votes and because more university graduates are needed for the new economic administrative plans, the standards are dropped. More BAs appear; but then as competition starts at the higher level something more is needed – a Master's degree or a Doctorate or (because the local degree is losing its prestige) a foreign degree.

It is difficult to expand an educational system rapidly without it going steadily downhill. The private universities in the Philippines are stigmatized as 'diploma mills' and in Japan as 'mass production universities'. There are other unfortunate side-effects in that the prestige of university education downgrades the status of the far more necessary technical education at post-secondary level. The result is a serious shortage of technicians and practical engineers, but a surplus of people with university degrees in agriculture and engineering. The graduates flock to the major cities and develop a style of living which makes the provinces seem unattractive. The gap between bureaucracy and peasantry, between rich and poor, between town and country, between university graduates and those who failed, grows wider and wider and makes a mockery of the egalitarian, socialist philosophy which inspired

Classroom scene at a Muslim school, Saiburi, South Thailand.

the educational expansion in the first place. A huge volume of additional pupils is poured into lower levels in order to obtain a handful of graduates and this uproots from the rural agricultural population a hundred times more children than can hope for jobs appropriate to graduates.

The Western system means high input, great wastage and low output. Gradually parents, even in remote villages, learn that school success means everything. Within a few years a deluge of children will complete primary school and a flood, smaller but more vocal, will complete secondary school. All will be determined to get away from agricultural occupations to work in a town. The oil refineries, steel works and already swollen government offices will not have jobs for all of them. The new educational system can so easily prepare the young for a way of life which cannot be provided. The end result of this is large numbers of partly-educated and dissatisfied young people with a larger number of 'have-nots' than 'haves'.

Thus education, which ought to be a blessing to people to teach them how to live, has become debased because it is seen only as a means to earn a living. Instead of producing more thoughtful and more intelligent literate people who will be more responsible citizens, it can so easily produce dissatisfaction, frustration and a desire to overthrow the existing government, not because it is a bad government, but solely in order to improve the material position of a new group.

The media

The electronic media, particularly television, have a deep effect upon people. I remember once trying to explain to Mangyan tribesmen in the Philippines how people in Singapore live in high-rise flats. Even though they themselves live only at subsistence level, they pitied the 'unfortunates' (as they saw them) in Singapore who have no land of their own on which to grow food. The fact that the average per capita income in Singapore would make them rich beyond their wildest dreams escaped them completely. Thai peasants with ample rice and protein derived from the flocks of ducks and shoals of fish are said to be basically happy and content.

Television, however, shows what others enjoy that we do not, and is thus potentially explosive in producing social discontent. People are able to see the wealth and recreation enjoyed by others. Television advertising operates on the principle of making people discontented with what they have got, and persuading people to want things which they have not got and which often they cannot afford. The impact of television therefore is often to make people discontented as they compare themselves with those in wealthier and more developed countries.

Marshall McLuhan divides human history into three periods. First there is illiterate Tribal Man, where knowledge is shared by a whole village community through verbal communication. Secondly, there is Gutenberg Man who, as a result of Gutenberg's invention of movable type, is able to gain information through reading books: all our early years are spent learning to read and write the symbols of learning, so

Escape from boredom takes many forms: television, the cinema, or (as here in Japan) the gaming-machines.

producing the modern education system. Thirdly, Electronic Man sees the whole world as a global village through the television screen.

In contemporary Asia we find all three kinds of people existing simultaneously. There are some who are already electronic men without ever having learned to read. They are still illiterate, but can understand the spoken words and pictures on the screen.

The scale of Japanese television has to be seen to be believed. In Tokyo there is a choice of six or seven channels operating in colour as well as others in black and white. Some programmes begin at six in the morning with soft music and nimble ladies encouraging us to take violent physical exercise. The influence of television upon language is remarkable. A new word has only to appear on a popular quiz programme to be in use throughout the country the following day. Television is a potent influence in giving people a total view of their own national society. It promotes the development of national languages and the absorption of ethnic minorities. In our earlier story of the Japanese searching for identity, television advertising had produced a stereotyped demand for goods and hence produced a monolithic culture.

The cinema in Asia is not being eclipsed by television as rapidly as in the West, for with crowded homes and the need for privacy, many young couples are looking for a quiet place to sit in the dark together. Thus horror films, sword fighting, pseudo-historical romances and even Japanese cowboy films are produced at a fantastic rate in all the main languages of the area. This is more on the level of entertainment than an art form. What intellectuals would regard as artistically excellent films are less popular with the masses. Huge garish posters of larger-than-life 'stars' are noticeable features of many Asian cities. Films and television seem to provide an escape from the drab monotony of everyday life in a technocratic society.

But are we just helpless victims of change? How free are we to decide whether we will change or not? Older people may resist change or deplore it, but the younger generation is conditioned by the changes to change still more. Is religion something which will help us to change?

Three

Religion as a Factor for Change

The previous chapters have shown that there are a whole variety of factors which are operating to produce rapid social change throughout Asia. In the past, religion has been a most significant factor in shaping history and attitudes to life in Europe and even more in Asia. In post-Christian Europe and America, religion has diminished considerably as an influence upon people in a secular age. Religious influence tends to conservatism, preserving the viewpoints and standards of the past. In Asia, however, the various Asian religions still have a powerful influence in Asian societies.

At the tribal level, animism still holds sway over the minds of simple country peasants who fear evil spirits thought to be responsible for illness and misfortune. They require the services of witch-doctors and shamans to provide sacrifices to placate the demons and thus to help them to survive trouble.

The truth is that animism is cruel to people. Animism keeps people in constant fear and hurts people economically. The few domestic animals are a much-needed source of protein, but have to be sacrificed to appease the spirits in times of sickness and disaster. Animism does not allow people to accept changes which would be beneficial to them. This is one of the main reasons for frequent breakdown of aid projects. People would rather go back to their old ways than use a technique which could offend the spirits.

Animistic ideas often survive in modified forms, even when more developed religions have theoretically superseded them. Trust in charms and fetishes and fear of spirits will be found mixed with Islam in Indonesia and Malaysia, with Buddhism in Thailand (and even in Japan), with Roman Catholicism in the Philippines and with Protestantism in Indonesia. Some more recent sects are little more than a re-mix of old ingredients, and frequently contain animistic elements.

The main religions of Asia

Islam has had a remarkable influence in East Asia, even though like Christianity it comes from the Far West of Asia. In Kuala Lumpur, you

Traditional religion and local culture are inextricably entwined. These carvings decorate the ornate houses in Sulawesi, Indonesia.

may see the beautiful mosques and Islamic architecture of buildings around the cricket pitch and pavilion (a legacy of British colonialism). Even the airport is built on beautiful Islamic architectural lines. In Singapore and in South Thailand, the Malay girls may be distinguished by their modestly concealing long garments, while Chinese and Thai girls prefer to follow current fashion.

The Koranic schools have been a major influence in education. The crowds of men cycling to the mosques on Fridays, the fast period of Ramadan, the black caps worn in Indonesia and white caps for those who have the distinction of having made the pilgrimage to Mecca, the ban on alcohol and pork, all illustrate the cultural impact of Islam. In the Philippine island of Mindanao, there has been repeated trouble between the Moro Muslims and the government. As the majority religion in Malaysia and Indonesia and the religion of significant separatist minorities both in the Philippines and in Thailand, its influence upon both cultural change and resistance to change is significant.

It could be argued that because of the underlying fatalism of Islam it inevitably becomes resistant to change. All manner of misfortunes may so easily be regarded as 'the will of Allah'. Such a philosophy is an understandable human response to the struggle for survival in the cruel and inhospitable desert. It could thus be used to justify the continuation of feudal systems of government. But there is no real reason why Islamic governments should not be progressive. Certainly the Islamic view of the state has tended to mean that Islam has been the unifying factor, even though at grass-roots level for ordinary people it has largely meant the avoidance of alcohol rather than a personal relationship with a personal God. It can of course be argued that Islam is predominantly a man's religion: on Fridays the roads are thronged with bicycles as all the men go to worship in the local mosques together.

Shoes are left behind as the devout enter a mosque at Kuching, Sarawak.

Buddhism tends to be mixed with underlying animistic superstitions,

Buddhist monks at Phnom Penh.

Opposite page: Joss-sticks lit to ward off evil spirits: a Chinese temple in Taiwan. Bottom: A night-long procession to rid a house of a demon.

Buddhist temples at Phnom Penh, Cambodia, and Utai, Thailand.

Buddhist monks (right and far right) at Nakon Sawan, Thailand, collecting alms.

A spirit house for a bank in Bangkok.

The Toraja burial-place at Rantilemo, Sulawesi, contains life-sized wooden models of the people buried.

An offering at a Chinese temple in Kaosiung, Taiwan (above), after an explosion in a house had killed many people. The devout light tapers (right) in a Chinese temple at Taipei, Taiwan. City-dwellers, hemmed in by buildings and traffic, turn to traditional answers in a modern context (far right), such as the 'demon shops', or spirit houses to keep away evil spirits: there is one on each staircase of these blocks of flats in modern Singapore.

Buddhist temple in Thailand.

Hindu temple at Kuala Lumpur, Malaysia.

Muslim mosque at Kuching,
Sarawak, East Malaysia.

Wives of Muslim dignitaries
arriving for a special occasion.

A new mosque (left) at Kuala Lumpur, Malaysia.

especially fear of the spirits of the dead. It has also been influential in producing a distinctive world-view. The individual's own thoughts and religious experience are the only reality; the world scene is regarded as an unreal image on the mental television screen of our own mind. This partly explains the passive inactivity and 'it doesn't matter' fatalism of the Thai and other peoples where Buddhist influence has been strong. On the other hand the temples of Thailand serve as community centres, clinics, libraries, recreation and health centres, thus performing a useful social function in the community.

In Japan, while theoretically the priest is a professional seeker for enlightenment, and the Buddhist sutras are intended to help the living to attain enlightenment, in the event the sutras are in a language incomprehensible to modern Japanese, and the living pay the priests to recite the sutras at funerals for the benefit of the spirits of the dead. It is not true Buddhism at all: the sutras are being used as a charm to keep the dead quiet!

It should be remembered that Gautama was looking for a solution to the problems of disease and death when stressing the concept that life is an illusion: it is a 'world of dew'. It is not clear that this particular solution to human suffering and death can satisfy any but the more stoical of human beings. When the last surviving child of the Japanese poet Issa died, his Buddhist friends gathered round to comfort him and to remind him that this was indeed a 'world of dew', that therefore both he and his child were unreal and so there was no point in his grieving over the passing of an illusion. Issa then penned the poignant lines, 'Tsuyu no yo wa tsuyu no yo nagara, sarinagara.'

Shinto shrine, Sapporo, Japan.

A worshipper prays and burns incense, Kuching, Sarawak.

It is never easy to give an adequate translation of one of these very brief Japanese poems but this will give the idea: 'The world of dew is a world of dew, and yet, and yet . . .' It expresses the deep longing in the human heart of any man, regardless of his religious background, for a continuing reality after death. It is not satisfying to regard those whom we love best as mere illusions passing through our consciousness. We long that they might be real and that somehow they might continue to exist, that there might be the possibility of our meeting them again. It is here perhaps that the Christian message of the resurrection of the dead has its particular appeal.

During the Pacific War when so many Japanese were dying for the emperor it would seem that the sense that a loved one had died for the national glory was more of a comfort to the bereaved than Buddhist thinking. Shinto seemed to carry more comfort than Buddhism at such a time. Significantly also the considerable number turning from Buddhism to Christianity in Phnom Penh in the last two or three years of the Vietnam war suggests that in times of agony and crisis, loss of property and life and the threat of death, the Buddhist solution is not always satisfying.

Curiously enough both Buddhism, where all things are part of the total reality of 'God', and Islam, where Allah is utterly separate from and far above men and all created things, are fatalistic systems. In Buddhism this is because what will happen will happen, and I have no responsibility for what happens. Thus, because I am not responsible for what happens, there is no ultimate distinction between good and evil. The qualities of resignation and extinction of desire are on the pathway to enlightenment. In Islam, man can only accept the inscrutable and irresistible will of Allah. Curiously, while Buddhism is all-inclusive and capable of infinite absorption of other ideas because of its world-view, Islam, like Christianity and Judaism, is intolerant of all other religions: yet both these Asian religions encourage a fatalistic resignation.

By contrast Confucianism, while more of a social philosophy than a religion (it worships no God and is chiefly concerned with social ethics), has been influential in making Chinese, Koreans and Japanese respect their ancestors and work industriously for the benefit of their parents and their descendants. It is responsible likewise for that apparently contradictory quirk of the Japanese character that makes him so industrious a worker while so subjective a thinker. Confucian thinking inculcates a deep sense of responsibility not only towards his own family, but to his superiors and society at large and supremely to the emperor. More recently the influence of existentialist and nihilist ideas from Europe has been eroding the traditional sense of responsibility.

Religion and change

It can be seen therefore that all these Asian religions have been significant in encouraging both cultural change and resistance to change. Whole cultures have been shaped by religion which influences the way

Tribal people, like these Orang Asli in the Cameron Highlands of West Malaysia, live in fear of spirits and depend on the traditional means of warding them off.

Worshippers make an offering in
a Chinese temple at Kaosiung,
Taiwan.

of thinking and approach to life of huge populations. At the same time, for most ordinary people, religion is not a living force but rather a matter of good luck, of custom, of marriage and funeral ceremonies. The foreign visitor who starts to ask questions about the ordinary belief of ordinary people in their daily lives is often confused and even distressed at the extreme vagueness of the reply which he receives. It would seem that religion has become more a matter of doing the right thing at the right time than anything really significant in determining human behaviour or providing an effective motivation for changing the world. Indeed, rather than changing and transforming mankind, it seems to be a way of making existing suffering bearable and explicable, of justifying the way things are, instead of being a living force to make things different.

Some Asian religions seem to have gained influence by absorbing or compromising with religious customs rather than sweeping them away. Both Christianity and Islam in the light of their essential beliefs are committed to the abolition of all the older superstitions, yet sadly they too have sometimes tended to a form of syncretism where many of the older beliefs or practices are preserved in a modified form. Of all the great religions Communism has perhaps been the most consistent in seeking to indoctrinate and to eliminate all other patterns of thinking. But should belief be spread by violent force and compulsory indoctrination? Or should it win its own way by the integrity with which the religion is practised by its adherents?

It is sometimes suggested that Christianity has been irresponsible in the cultural changes it has produced and that its messengers, in their desire to change beliefs, have tended to ride roughshod over indigenous cultures. We have already seen, however, that cultures are changing all the time, as a result of many different factors including religious ones. Among the various religious influences upon culture, the Christian message in Asia has had far less influence than Hinduism, Buddhism, Islam and Confucianism.

That the whole world is experiencing rapid social change is very obvious. Some people certainly are endeavouring to manipulate and direct that change in the direction they feel desirable. But as Roszak puts it, 'If the melancholy history of revolution over the past half century teaches us anything it is the futility of a politics which concentrates itself single-mindedly on the overthrowing of Governments, or ruling classes, or economic systems. This brand of politics finishes with merely redesigning the turrets and towers of the technocratic citadel.'

All of us are afraid that change has got out of control, that nobody is really in charge. Everyone feels that society is 'going down the drain' and that politicians are arguing about the shape of the plug-hole! None of us wants to end up under that plastic tree with a programmed grin on our face. We share the anxiety of the Japanese commuter lest we end up as a group of well-conditioned ants in a huge technocratic ant-heap.

Is Christianity just another ancient Asian religion, or can it possibly be the new society for which we are searching?

Four

The Missionaries

Many of the early European settlers and missionaries died of disease or were put to death. These graves at an old church in Malacca date from the seventeenth century.

There have been Christians in Asia for two thousand years: not only initially in Palestine but in Egypt and Syria, in Ethiopia and North Africa. The Christian faith spread from Syria to South India and even to China through the Nestorian Christians. Later, the Roman Catholic Jesuit missionaries such as Francis Xavier took the Christian message to Goa, Malacca, Vietnam, China, the Philippines and Japan. They were courageous men, for one in every three of them died of disease or through

shipwreck on the way – and when they did arrive they were often persecuted and put to death. In the last hundred years, however, we have seen many new Christian congregations started, often in the face of prejudice, opposition and persecution.

Missionaries these days are no longer necessarily white Europeans or Americans. Within the Overseas Missionary Fellowship, for example, there are missionaries from Japan, Korea, Philippines, Hong Kong, Singapore, Malaysia, India and Fiji, and Maoris from New Zealand. The Korean church has a missionary tradition almost as long as its history. Teams from Indonesia have travelled widely, not only throughout the archipelago, but beyond to South Thailand and other places. Thus it is no longer Western churches only which send out missionaries. Asian churches too are sending out their own members in increasing numbers to help in other parts of the world.

It may well be that America and Europe will increasingly receive missionaries from the rest of the world. A cheerful group of guitar-playing Filipinos might well be more effective as missionaries in down-town Liverpool, Amsterdam or Chicago than some of the professional clergy in middle-class churches. When this starts to happen, some of the cultural problems will appear in reverse, as missionaries from Japan and Korea unconsciously bring with them things which are products of their own cultures rather than intrinsic to basic biblical Christianity. The fact

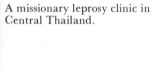

A missionary leprosy clinic in Central Thailand.

that modern missionaries come from a variety of nationalities indicates the universality of Christianity.

Missionaries today and yesterday

Missionaries today may be found in unlikely places. A number work in universities, making a contribution to Asian life through lecturing in their specialist subjects as well as by communicating their Christian faith to others. One missionary is working on a cheap television receiver for signals directly from satellites; others may be teaching soil science, marine biology, surgery, human genetics or solid state physics.

The word 'missionary' still conjures up for many the intrepid explorer – like Livingstone – hacking his way through the impenetrable jungle, and wearing a topee. These days the missionary is more likely to be found wearing a crash-helmet (a legal requirement in many Asian countries when riding motorbikes), a surgeon's cap in the operating-room, a flying-helmet when piloting an aeroplane, an academic mortar-board at a graduation, or earphones as he makes radio or television programmes.

It has become fashionable in recent years to caricature missionaries as somewhat ridiculous Victorian figures. While nineteenth-century missionaries were inevitably people of their own time, it is indisputable that the pioneer missionaries were a heroic lot. The early Protestant missionaries made long voyages of up to a year in sailing ships and arrived wearing the cumbersome, long and unhealthy, heavy clothing of nineteenth-century Europe and America. They were without protective inoculations, anti-malarial drugs, antiseptics or antibiotics and consequently they had a very short expectation of life. It was commonplace for young wives to die in childbirth and for their children to be carried off in infancy by epidemics.

Of the early missionaries in Siam (Thailand) some sixty or more died within a few years of arrival of endemic malaria, cholera, typhus and other fevers. Small wonder that progress was slow. They laboured for nineteen years before seeing their first convert, and he was a Chinese! Many died before they could give a clear explanation of the Christian faith in the indigenous language. And yet, astonishingly, replacements continued to come forward and to work selflessly in the heat until they dropped, in their efforts to establish Christian congregations.

In 1810, two long lifetimes ago, William Carey proposed a World Missions Conference. This never took place because in the days of sailing ships it was somewhat impractical to gather everybody together in the Cape of Good Hope. In any case there was only the tiniest handful of Protestant missionaries in the whole of Africa, Asia and Latin America. Today there are Christian churches in every country of the Third World apart from Mauretania in Africa and the Mongolian People's Republic in Asia. This remarkable change has taken place in the past century and a half.

It is often thought that missionary work made progress only because it was sponsored by colonial governments as the religion of the

Missionaries 'plant' or start new congregations: an old church building dating from Portuguese Catholic and Dutch Protestant days in Djakarta contrasts with one in a rural area of East Malaysia. Reminders of former days (below) remain in the Taroko Gorge, Taiwan: the memorial church to a Tatal woman evangelist and the cave where Christians met secretly for fear of the Japanese colonial government.

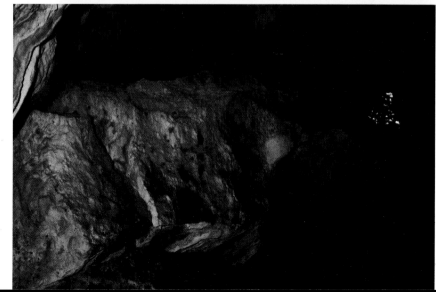

Teaching, speaking, listening, sitting where people sit, explaining the Christian good news: left, a Bible study group in Southern Thailand. The pictures below show (top, left) a house-church in the same area, and (top, right) a missionary visiting a former leprosy patient of the Manorom Hospital, further north in Central Thailand. Centre: A German missionary at work in the Kaosiung factory girls' hostel, Taiwan (left); and a Malay church in Southern Thailand. Bottom: In the Philippines, a school for the local Alangan tribe is held in the missionary's home in Mindoro (left); leadership training (right) is given to church leaders of the Hanunoo tribe.

Getting down to language study (above) at Sapporo, Japan. A Swiss missionary (right) enjoys Japanese food! And in the Philippines the mission truck takes a flooded road – travel methods vary from jet to foot-slogging, with every variation in between.

What it means to be a missionary today: a missionaries' child looks out of their apartment window to the high-rise buildings of Hong Kong.

Christian concern for East Asia has been a major factor in establishing medical facilities, pioneering treatment for illnesses such as leprosy, and setting up hospitals in remoter areas which are unattractive to doctors compared with the highly paid jobs in the cities, but where medical services are badly needed. Two Christian doctors at Masan, Korea (left), join in prayer for the day's work. Youngsters suffering from hip and spinal tuberculosis are helped at the Masan Clinic (below), and a former leprosy patient (bottom) is back at work near Utai, Thailand. A missionary nurse at Saiburi Christian Hospital, Thailand, helps a child back to health (opposite).

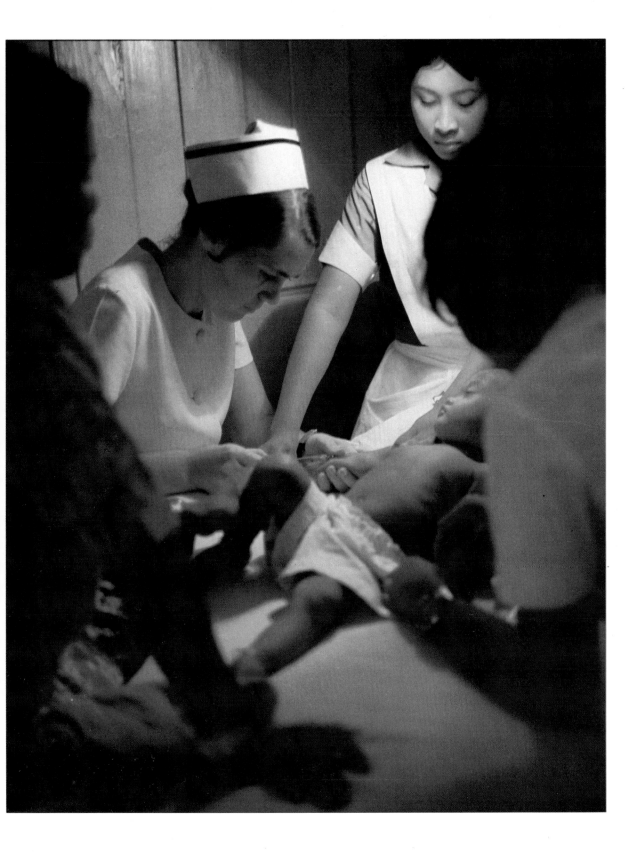

THE MISSIONARIES / 81

Ouch! Danger, missionary at work . . . tackling the physical as well as the spiritual needs of the White Meo tribe of Thailand.

establishment. But in Asia, countries such as Thailand and Japan were never under colonial powers at all. And elsewhere colonial governments were not always particularly helpful to Christianity. Frequently Christian missionaries were discouraged, as a potential threat to trade because they might cause religious unrest. William Carey was not allowed to work in British India at all and was based on the Danish Colony of Serampore. In Malaya, under the British, it was forbidden to preach to the Malays. The Dutch East India Company for many years forbade missionary work among the Javanese lest it provoke trouble. This regulation was revoked during the latter period of Dutch rule, but the astonishing growth of the Christian church in Indonesia has occurred since independence and the ending of colonial rule.

The identification of Christianity with Western powers has rarely been helpful. In Japan, Christianity was seriously hindered because it always seemed to arrive under the umbrella of foreign aggression. The earlier Roman Catholic missionaries arriving with the Spanish and Portuguese traders (who also brought the musket) were finally bloodily suppressed. The Protestants first came in when the gunboat diplomacy of Commodore Parry's 'black ships' forced Japan to open its ports to Western trade. After some initial progress, Christianity was rejected by Emperor-worshipping militarism. The churches were oppressed and harassed during the Pacific War, after which a new wave of missionaries arrived under the sponsorship of General MacArthur, as supreme commander of the occupying forces. It is not surprising, then, that Christianity still suffers in Japan, because it is thought of as a foreign religion from America and Europe.

In Korea, by contrast, Christianity grew because the church was identified with resistance to the Shinto religion of the hated colonial Japanese power. Young patriots saw the church as the bastion of nationalistic resistance to the foreigner. Today the church in Korea is proportionately the strongest and largest anywhere in Asia, approaching three million Christians in a country of thirty million.

The missionary at work

But what about missionaries today? What are they trying to achieve? They are often accused of upsetting and altering ancient cultures. But, as we have already seen, there are innumerable factors changing culture very rapidly and Christianity is only one small element. It has probably caused far less disturbance than the other religions which have come into East Asia from further West: Hinduism and Buddhism from India and Islam from the Arab world. The impact of Western technology and Western political theory, especially Marxism, has been a much more significant factor.

The modern missionary is concerned to identify with the people in the culture to which he goes. He lives in the normal style of housing of ordinary people. He eats the food of the country and, of course, he speaks its language. Inevitably he shares also in the suffering which comes through floods, typhoons, earthquakes, epidemics and war.

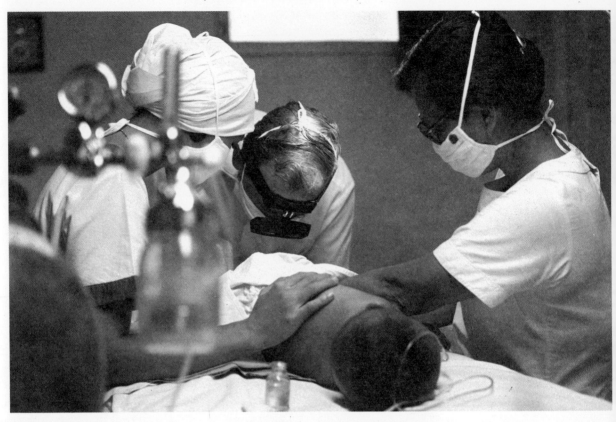

Surgery at the Saiburi Hospital in South Thailand.

Some think of missionaries as working for basically humanitarian reasons, a form of religious philanthropy, spiritual 'do-gooders'. They are thought of simply as exponents of the ethic of 'never to do anybody any harm'!

The purpose of missionary work may be stated simply as the four stages of preaching and teaching, planting and perfecting congregations. It is not just to do good, although that in itself is beneficial to mankind and glorifying to God. It is not just to propagandize and advertise Christianity through the distribution of leaflets and literature explaining the content of Christian belief. Nor is it merely to make converts, people who will call themselves Christians. It is rather so to teach and preach and lead individuals to a living faith in Christ, that new congregations are started and these are then perfected as new Christian communities. If these are little more than imitations of the weekly 'religious observance' type of Christianity found in the West, they are of minimal use. People have little time for such passive, once-a-week spectator Christianity. The aim is rather to build new communities in the middle of the old decaying societies.

The role of the Christian missionary in changing Asian communities has therefore been mainly indirect – although as people become Christians and change their attitudes and beliefs, they change their behaviour too. But the missionaries' role has also been active. Because of their concern for the people around them, and as an expression of the Christian gospel, they have tackled vital areas of human need in a spirit of dedication and service.

Medical missionary work has always been a particularly Christian contribution not characteristic of other world religions. It was Christians who were the first to bring hospitals and leprosaria to Asia, in days before national governments accepted responsibility for such work. This was possible partly because the period of Protestant missionary activity coincided with advances in medical technology, which societies such as the Leprosy Mission were able to apply. The first use of anaesthesia and smallpox vaccination in Thailand (and probably anywhere in the Far East) was by the missionary Dr Samuel House. Often Christian missionaries have been tolerated in countries initially hostile or suspicious of the message they brought, precisely because of the medical services they offered, at a time when other medical services were inadequate. Christian doctors and nurses were prepared to leave their own home countries, their friends and families, the comfort and security of their homelands and more lucrative employment in order to serve needy people for the sake of Christ.

Strangely, because of human greed, this still remains a missionary contribution, because doctors, pharmacists and others making a living

Nurse and patient share a joke at the Masan Hospital, Korea.

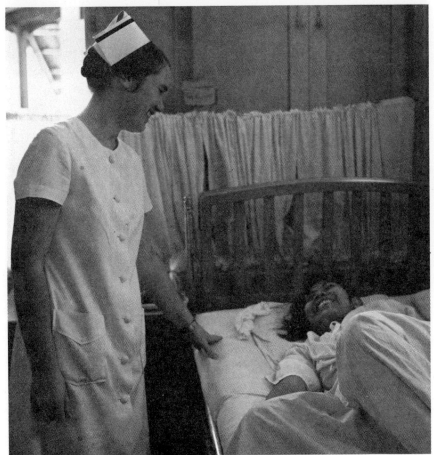

From here two women, Overseas Missionary Fellowship missionaries, were kidnapped, taken and held for ransom, and later put to death.

out of other people's diseases tend to congregate in the largest cities where money can be made from the rich, rather than facing the difficulty of working in poorer provincial areas. Thus missionaries are still making a real medical contribution in remoter areas. They treat the disease of leprosy, they rehabilitate through constructive surgery to make hands and feet usable again, and they provide occupational therapy to teach people a new trade and enable them to regain their self-respect. They also teach them about the human dignity that God has given to mankind and about eternal life and new bodies in the new creation. The two Overseas Missionary Fellowship nurses who were taken captive for ransom and subsequently shot were treating poverty-stricken sufferers from leprosy in the extreme south of Thailand.

Because of the tendency of professional people to concentrate in the big cities, the need in the countryside may well continue for some time to depend upon the contribution of such voluntary medical agencies. But as governments are more and more able to provide good medical services, the medical missionary contribution will become less and less necessary. An OMF missionary doctor in Korea makes his particular contribution through a hospital providing free treatment for children suffering from tuberculosis of the hip and spine. This is the only hospital in the whole country providing free in-patient treatment for the children of the poor, who otherwise suffer a lifetime with their limbs totally immobilized.

Social concern

Some Christians have made a contribution through agricultural work, although such services are also provided through other voluntary agencies such as the Peace Corps and Voluntary Service Overseas. This is probably just as well, for there is always the danger that such help may be thought of as offering inducements to conversion. In the last century so-called 'Rice Christians' in China saw membership of the church as a form of insurance against famine, so that they would benefit from Christian aid and missionary hand-outs. The Chinese Viceroy in Tientsin, Li Hung-Chang, remarked to Timothy Richard in 1880, 'Should mercenary advantages be withdrawn from the so-called Christian converts of the poor and lowly ignorant lower classes there would soon be no more Christians in China . . .'

There is still a danger that one result of practical Christian help is that adherents appear to be added to the congregation, but are not really converted to Christianity at all. The attraction is rather Western technology. They are rescued from the frying-pan of primitive super-stitions and taboos, only to land in the fire of materialism. The benefits offered are not really the benefits of Christianity, apart from the altruistic kindness of those who introduce them, so much as products of Western technological society. This inevitably brings with it many other problems such as affluence, greed, alcoholism, gambling and crime.

The balance is probably best where the Christian doing other work is able to give incidental help. A Swiss missionary with agricultural training teaches in the tribal Bible School in Mindoro. When tribes-people reported a crop failure, he was able to go up and assess the situation and recommend an insecticide to eradicate the grub destroying plants in the area, and also suggest fertilizer and seed which would be helpful. Having given the technical advice, he was then able to return to his normal work.

Leprosy patient, Korea.

Agricultural work at Mindoro, Philippines.

Both missionaries and national Christians can express their social concern. Social justice is not always appreciated as much as it might be: it is still said in some Asian countries that the spider's web of the law only catches the smaller flies, while the bigger influential ones are always able to pay their way to freedom.

In the Philippine island of Mindoro, the aboriginal Mangyan were constantly losing mountain land which they had cleared and cultivated from the jungle to unscrupulous landgrabbing lowlanders. The missionaries preaching to the aboriginal people took their part and were able to enlist the help of Christian lowlanders. A group of these men formed the Philippines Christian Lawyers' Fellowship, and give their time and energy to helping these impoverished people rather than making money out of the wealthy in the great city of Manila. More recently this same group has initiated a social development programme for the mountain people with generous aid from the churches of Germany. Such assistance is not 'bait' to persuade people to accept the Christian gospel, but rather the 'fruit' of consistent national Christians developing a care for their less fortunate neighbours.

Social protest

Most people are familiar with the fact that it was the Scottish missionary, David Livingstone, who first roused the Christian conscience to see the guilt of the white men on the West Coast and of the Arabs on the East Coast of Africa, carrying Africans into slavery.

It is less well known that Christians were involved in constant protest and lobbying against the evils of the Opium Trade. As early as 1843, Lord Shaftesbury moved a resolution in the House of Commons:

'That it is the opinion of this House that the continuance of the trade in opium, and the monopoly of its growth in the territories of British India, are destructive of all relations of amity between England and China, injurious to the manufacturing interests of the country by the very serious dimunition of legitimate commerce and utterly inconsistent with the honour and duties of a Christian kingdom: and that steps should be taken, as soon as possible, with due regard to the rights of Government and individuals to abolish the evil.'

In 1856, the Annual Report of the Edinburgh Medical Missionary Society proposed a motion condemning the Opium trade between the British Indies and China. It was noted that opium had been annually exported from India to China, valued at about £7 million and this was being introduced into China in opposition to the laws of that empire:

'This contraband has seriously affected the extension of friendly relations with China and is being carried by professing Christians, is throwing discredit on the Christian religion, and is seriously retarding the progress of the Christian religion in that Empire.'

For much of its early history, the China Inland Mission did its utmost to acquaint the Christian public with what was happening. In the preface to the bound volume of its magazine *China's Millions* in 1878, the mission's founder, Hudson Taylor, mentions the opium traffic on the

A Christian lawyer in the Philippines (standing, right) at a court-case. Christian Lawyers' Fellowship members acted on behalf of the poor, aboriginal people in the mountains.

very first page and comments:

'The Christian missionary has no greater hindrance to his usefulness than the prejudice excited against him on account of our country's connection with the Opium Trade.'

In the index under the heading 'O', there are no less than ten entries for that one year on the subject of Opium traffic, including a series of eight letters accompanied by black-and-white drawings of opium smoking and the suffering caused by it. An article is included by no less a person than His Excellency, the Prime Minister of the Chinese Empire, and also a letter from the Chinese Ambassador, Kuo Sung-Tao from Langham Place, London.

The same issue also contained accounts of famine in China, accompanied by lurid drawings of what famine means, showing cannibalism, suicide and death by starvation. The CIM did not hesitate to point out that the total amount given that year for famine relief in China (some £40,000) was equivalent to the profit gained by Britain from opium in two days. The same volume contained no less than twenty-five references in the course of the year and covering several pages on the subject of famine relief. These facts in themselves are enough to show that nineteenth-century missionaries, although children of their time,

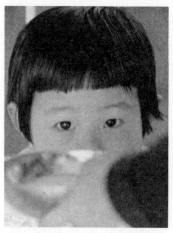

Christians have been active in the need to improve nutritional standards and provide food for the undernourished.

were not so entirely taken up with preaching the gospel of eternal life in the next world, that they were not also deeply concerned about seeking to help people in this world and particularly to ameliorate the effect of famines and social injustice that were increasing the suffering of the Chinese people.

In *China's Millions* as late as 1901, under the heading 'The Greatest Crime of the Century', there is a diagram of a clock indicating that on average a ton of opium had been exported to China during every two hours of Queen Victoria's Sixty Glorious Years.

A retired Director of the China Inland Mission, Benjamin Broomhall, started a magazine *National Righteousness* attacking the opium traffic to China and the drink trade to Africa. Copies of the magazine were sent to all Members of Parliament, and meetings and special breakfasts were held in order to lobby for an end to the traffic.

This social protest was directed not to Asian rulers, but to the missionaries' own home governments. Today when missionaries are guests of governments, tolerated on entry visas which can easily be revoked, they are, of necessity, silent about social issues of the country in which they are guests. National Christians, however, are able to make such protests to their own governments. Before the Communist takeover in Vietnam, Christians were demonstrating against social injustice in their own country.

Community health

Some people remember Rousseau's idealized 'noble savage' living in primeval splendour, uncorrupted by civilization. As the story of the Lun Bawang tribe (see page 118) indicates, the truth is very different. We find societies which are seriously deprived, dying in misery of malnutrition and disease, and living in superstitious fear of taboos, omens and evil spirits.

The teaching of missionaries has sometimes assisted government programmes to help such people. The official public health scheme for the Tagal people made little headway until they embraced Christianity. Tagal custom placed a taboo on the eating of green vegetables by any woman who was pregnant or breast-feeding babies. In tribal culture, a woman normally continued breast-feeding one child until the next was born. In effect, therefore, this meant that once a girl became pregnant, she was not allowed to eat green vegetables until she finished her child-bearing career. This resulted in a very serious anaemia. Often these people were living for years with a haemoglobin level around 25 per cent, which would certainly put a Westerner totally out of action. With such severe chronic anaemia, resistance to disease was very low; pneumonia was a disease which killed mothers and children within twelve hours.

One possibility was for the doctor to try somehow to reach all pneumonia cases before they died. This was an impossible programme for a community of 22,000 in a mountainous area. Another possibility would have been to treat the anaemia by giving iron tablets, a relatively low-cost programme. In fact the medical problem was solved by Christian

Manorom Christian Hospital in Central Thailand gives an opportunity for the practical demonstration of Christian concern in a Buddhist environment.

One of the leprosy clinics at nearby Utai.

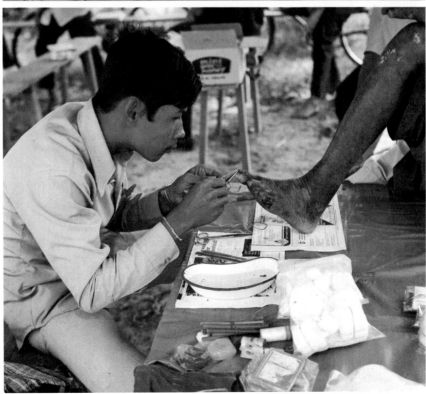

Faith and farming: a missionary
agriculturalist combines teaching
and agricultural work at
Mayabig, Philippines.

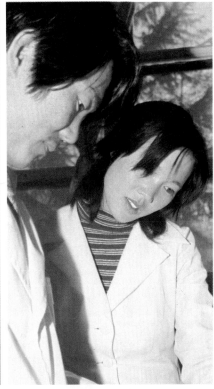

Missionaries today tackle a
variety of jobs, expressing their
faith in action, working alongside
others and helping the people
they have come to serve. An OMF
missionary teaches electronics
(top left) at Hong Kong
University, working on satellite
communications. Medical staff
(right) are at the Masan Clinic,
Korea. A Physics lecturer
demonstrates an experiment at
the Medan University, Sumatra
(lower, left); and a missionary
teaches leprosy patients in South
Thailand to rear chicks, to help
increase their income.

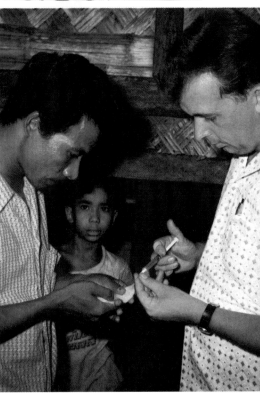

Different situations call for different forms of missionary outreach. Young people sing in a coffee shop in Japan (right). A student group meets in Manila, Philippines (top). The ship *Logos* takes an educational book exhibition and video and other training aids (above) from port to port.

Teaching, that they may teach others. In the Philippines a missionary (above) discusses visual aids with the teacher before the Bible story session (right).

Prayer before an open-air baptism in the Philippines.

evangelism. Tagal people who became Christians were no longer subject to the taboos. In the context of the co-operative community of the church congregation, they were encouraged to eat green vegetables and this resulted in higher haemoglobin levels and the eradication of pneumonia as a killing disease. The result of Christian preaching was a healthy community.

The same group was also subject to venereal disease. Before the British administration came, there were strong social sanctions against illegitimate births. The child, the mother and the man responsible were all put to death. The British administration (understandably) decided that this was rather too drastic and so the penalty of a small fine was substituted.

The men had little to do, became addicted to alcohol and, in the absence of severe sanctions, became sexually promiscuous. There was general promiscuity, including teenagers. After a while, there were no children under the age of twenty. Children were just not being born. Promiscuity was transmitting an anaerobic staphylococcus which blocked the women's fallopian tubes so that they became sterile and incapable of having children. One result of the conversion of the tribes to Christianity was that promiscuity was dealt with and the disease was checked.

A non-Christian government medical dresser commented that the Christian tribal people in the fourth and fifth Divisions of Sarawak showed a much greater responsiveness than others to government health schemes, and the cleanliness of their villages was remarkable.

Among the many social pressures to which the aboriginal mountain people are subjected in the Philippines is that which insists that certain behaviour is 'civilized' while other behaviour is not. In the nineteenth century some of the Western missionaries encouraged converts to wear clothes. These days missionaries interfere with cultures as little as they can, and often oppose the social pressures to imitate so-called 'civilized' clothing habits.

Tribal children attending lowland schools are required to wear clothes, and adults trading in the towns find themselves despised for their uncivilized 'G-string' culture. In some areas they are not allowed into town without a shirt. However, clothes rapidly become dirty in the mountains, where soap is often not available, and in the humid forests, with daily rainfall, it is remarkably difficult to dry clothes properly. In no time the clothes take on a greyish hue and are often put on again without being properly dried. Consequently, the wearers catch cold, and may develop coughs and pneumonia, because malnutrition makes them susceptible to infection. In the jungle it is much healthier *not* to wear clothes. Thus missionaries today would rather encourage them to retain their traditional undress than slavishly to imitate the habits of the lowlanders. Missionaries sometimes encourage mountain preachers who have adopted Western-style dress to go back to the G-string, lest they be rejected because of associating Christianity with the lowland culture.

Missionaries and local cultures

The contribution missionaries make in preserving tribal cultures is often overlooked. In many countries, they are the only people who can address

The missionary adopts traditional local dress to speak with people in the village meeting-place, Toraja.

tribal people in their own language. Government officials, often with the difficult task of implementing a policy of integrating racial minorities, address the tribesmen in the national language, which the people are expected to learn. Missionaries, on the other hand, learn the tribal language as quickly as possible and then labour for years analysing the language, producing dictionaries and some form of phonetic script and then teaching tribal people to read their own language, in order that they may read the Bible in their own tongue. Were it not for missionaries most of these languages would never have been preserved in writing at all, and people would never have been literate in their tribal tongue. A significant result of this work is to preserve language groups. Among the Yao tribe, a missionary has recorded the song cycles of the people in order to gain a greater understanding of their culture. In Thailand also, Thai script has been used for tribal translations so that tribal people can not only learn to read their own language, but the national language as well.

In Mindoro, missionary Ann Flory ran crash courses for groups of young men in order that they might return to their villages and bring the next generation of children into literacy. The effect of these very simple primary schools was, of course, to change Tribal men into Gutenberg men.

Thus missionaries may co-operate with desirable social change, or even help to accelerate it in the interest of the underprivileged minority, who are otherwise at a serious disadvantage because they cannot read or write.

One problem of being a missionary is that you have to be born somewhere! So you may unconsciously export ideas and customs which are a product of your own culture and are not necessarily intrinsic to biblical Christianity. Tourists viewing Singapore Cathedral may rightly wonder how a Singaporean could possibly be an Anglican by conviction! It is hard to know what a Southern Baptist is doing in Northern Japan!

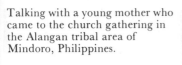

Talking with a young mother who came to the church gathering in the Alangan tribal area of Mindoro, Philippines.

Young and old crowd into a hymn-singing session, Saba, Sarawak. Indonesian hymns reveal their Dutch heritage, despite efforts to bring in music more suited to the strong local culture.

Such Western denominations are the results of local historical situations in their own countries.

Sometimes missionaries do export things which are purely cultural: thus America has exported to the Philippines song-leaders, pianos and organs playing together, and even times of services. In the tropics, it is foolish to follow the Western habit of holding services in the late forenoon when people feel both sleepy and hungry: early morning is much more logical.

It would be ridiculous to assert that there have not been some bad practitioners among missionaries. We are all children of our own time. However, just as it would be ridiculous to write off all medical practitioners because a few doctors have been ignorant or mercenary, so also it would be unjust to suggest that all missionaries have been culturally clueless. The Indonesian churches among the Bataks in Sumatra and in Toraja in the Celebes show their own distinctive architecture, and their church buildings are uniquely products of their own culture. In Sarawak, the longhouses remain. It is imitation of other people on the coast, rather than the church policy, which accounts for the tendency of some to begin to live in small, independent homes. Modern missionaries are acutely conscious, if they have been properly trained and prepared, of the need for avoiding cultural imperialism. The magazine *Practical Anthropology* has been given up almost entirely to considering problems of cross-cultural communication put by missionaries.

Some problems are difficult to solve. Few of us can write good hymns, even in our own language, with tunes for them using traditional melodies in octaves. Very few missionaries could write acceptable hymns in other languages, still less write pentatonic music for them. Thus, inevitably, new churches begin with poor translations of Western hymns sung to the Western tunes familiar to the missionaries. It is only later that national Christians start to write original hymns with indigenous music. Thailand Christians especially enjoy such locally written hymns to pentatonic music. Muslim converts in South Thailand use Bible verses set to indigenous melodies.

In a quiet way, then, Christian missionaries prove to have been a powerful and interesting illustration of how change in Asia can come about: not by revolution or violent takeover, trampling on previously-held beliefs or cultures, but by changing people, changing the beliefs which mould people's lives.

But it is the convictions they have brought which have proved so powerful, not their methods. They are convictions which demand closer study.

Five

New Communities of the New Humanity

As we have read and looked at pictures of Asia and seen the rapid changes, we may have wondered where all this is leading. It is moving towards the same technological tyranny as is suffered by the industrial nations of Europe and America? Are the masses of Asia to be manipulated and programmed prisoners of material affluence? How can man in Asia find identity in a society which becomes increasingly overcrowded, where everyone is programmed by the mass media to become more and more alike? How can we escape the drab monotony of everyday life in such a mass consumer society?

There has been a plan to restructure Hong Kong on three levels with industry at ground level, shopping centres on the middle level and residential areas built up above the other two. Men are beginning to live like ants, industriously building themselves huge synthetic ants' nests. How different from the agricultural way of life which this is replacing!

What kind of life-style will be offered to the children of Asia? Is it to be this depersonalized alienation, where the individual feels an insignificant cog in a huge impersonal machine?

The main factor in change is people: if you change the people, you can change the world. What we want is new values, a new outlook on life, a new quality of life beyond mere pointless affluence to fill the vacuum left by the loss of the old ways of life. Where will we find them?

As we have seen, it is an unproved assumption of Marxism that man becomes unselfish when his economic needs are met. The United States has the highest standard of living of any country in the world and yet has more delinquency, crime, drugs, murders and suicides. Mere affluence does not bring a contented society. Certainly it helps if we have enough to feed and clothe our bodies. But wealth alone does not seem to make people happy.

The countries of Asia are hurrying forward in a competitive rush towards . . . what? It is comparatively easy to encourage nations to pull themselves together and work hard to recover from the ravages of war. It is much harder to motivate people who are already relatively affluent. The affluent society becomes so pointless and people begin asking hard questions, asking to what end their children are being educated and for what they are working and being entertained, and what they will have to offer to their children after them . . .

Some Western young people have 'dropped out', sought to escape from such purposeless affluence and the manipulated world of the technocrats into the subjective experience offered by psychedelic drugs or the Zen Buddhism popularized by Alan Watts. Asian countries have resisted this 'counter-culture' for obvious reasons. Monastic withdrawal and opium-dreaming were tried long ago in Asia and found to be a non-solution for society as a whole. It is a pathetic non-solution to escape by withdrawal into one's own mind in the search for reality. Have I nothing better with which to measure the universe than the little understanding that I have of it myself?

Solutions

What we need is a solution which enables us to find fulfilment of our unique personalities as individuals, and yet to find them enriched by other personalities in a human community of richness and meaning. As we perspire in tropical heat, a refreshing breath of wind reminds us that coolness is possible. Behind a pile of cheap, mass-produced goods, products of this technocratic age, we suddenly see a priceless and unique object of skilled craftsmanship. In the midst of people who slavishly follow the advertisements and do what everybody else does, we occasionally meet an individual who is delightfully different and who refuses to follow the crowd.

Is a different way of life possible?

I recently met a wonderful community in the jungles of Sarawak. I had been down by the river, watching small boys swimming against the

Aerial view of a Lio Matu longhouse.

A rural church in the Philippines.

strong brown currents and playing adventurously in the canoes, almost amphibious in their conquest of water. Having washed ourselves in the river, we sat in the cool of the evening on the long veranda that joined the seventy doors of a Kayan longhouse housing seven hundred people. The older folk sat in the dusk, sitting as they say 'on the same bench' with others.

The scene reminded me of an old Dutch painting by Breughel: people returning from bathing, hunting or carrying bananas; children leaping over bamboo sticks, or skipping with rattan: there was not a mass-produced toy in sight. There was no sign of quarrelling or voices raised in anger. I was reminded of what the old Israelite prophet, Zechariah, saw in his vision: 'Old men and old women shall again sit in the streets: and the streets of the city shall be full of boys and girls playing in the streets . . .'

I have stayed in many countries in many homes for many weekends, but I have never enjoyed such a welcome as they gave us there. Where else would a visitor be given a new name, adopted into the family and made to feel he really belonged? They no longer treated us suspiciously as foreigners and strangers, but as fellow members of the longhouse, as members of the household of God.

Yes, this was a Christian longhouse now: earlier they had been head-hunters, and subject to many of the problems of tribal areas. Now they were an attractive new community. They had had all the problems of headhunting, malnutrition, alcoholism, promiscuity. Now they had become a Christian community. Nothing could be more different, however, from the 'Sunday congregation' kind of Christianity where people hardly know one another.

The Christian solution is being tried in Asia today and not found wanting, because it is seen as being genuinely a corporate rather than a

Though local cultures may be encouraged or preserved by missionaries, some practices fall away under the influence of the new faith. This Kuching girl was tattoed at the age of three by the cruel and painful process of inserting kerosene soot under the skin.

solitary religion. It starts by changing individuals, certainly. But it goes on to transform whole families and whole communities.

A Japanese Prime Minister a few years ago coined the slogan: 'From the change of the individual to the transformation of the nation.' In the second century, people spoke of Christians as 'the third race', the first being the Greek and the second the Jewish. Today in Asia, the Christian way is beginning to be seen as a third option to capitalist materialism or Communism. Both those systems press us remorselessly into their own preconditioned moulds. Both of them in their own well-meaning ways would take away our freedom. But the Christian answer calls for a new humanity, new people living together in new communities. It is not just a solitary salvation of the individual with God, but a communal, corporate salvation that begins to transfigure human existence on earth and transforms human relationships in preparation for the new heaven and the new earth. A new relationship with God must mean a new relationship with our neighbours.

Many other Asian religions, apart from Christianity, have offered individual religious experience, and some kind of ultimate salvation, but the concept of a 'redeemed people of God' is confined to Judaism (which often misunderstood it as exclusivism) and Christianity (which in the West has tended to overlook this and become selfishly individualistic). Both of these religions worship the same God and are in origin as Asian as Buddhism and Hinduism. When the Christianity of the Bible is simply understood, without the accretions of medieval European superstition and custom, it has a clear and welcome message for Asia.

Understanding Christianity

The starting-point for any understanding of Christianity must be the Bible, its source-document. There we read of God as the one who created all things, who created man because he wanted to share in fellowship with him. But we read too of man choosing evil, becoming an alien from the loveliness of God, preferring to go his own self-centred way. So God came into the world in person. He became a human being in order to be the prototype of a new humanity. It was not that God disguised himself as a human being, nor yet that he put his own divine Spirit into a human body. Jesus Christ was both God and man, and did not cease being either. He was born a man in an actual place at an actual time. He became man in order that other men might be restored to a relationship with God and become 'partakers of the divine nature'.

A Christian can be defined as a Christ-in person, someone who has God indwelling him. God is in us, transforming our lives daily, bringing us into a relationship with other individuals who have similarly entered into this new relationship with God. This brings into existence a new community of Christ-people, a congregation. They need not be living together in one house, like the Christian longhouse dwellers of Sarawak. They may be scattered throughout other communities, living in high-rise apartments in Hong Kong or Singapore, or in farming

ASIYA
— ha hayo, ham
— Ham
— hayo
gi hayo, giwa hayo
ham, hayo
PALESTINA
← tisalonika
Diyos intam
Panginoon Hisos
In Diyos Fiya Fag
Panginoon, Fiya Fag
fadowasay Masidoniya hanggan Akaya
bohondi sinya
— Pananampalataya
— pag-ibig
— pagasa
Masidoniya hanggan Akaya

The church meets: for a Sunday
school in the Philippines (left);
in a Sarawak longhouse (right);
to discuss publishing projects in
Hong Kong (below)

The church at work (left) : at the Ranau Bible School, Saba (top left) ; Filipino students at a Bible study (top right) ; leading the singing at a church in Korea ; a Filipino missionary 'planting' a new congregation in Japan ; a service in a refugee church (bottom left) in war-torn Phnom Penh ; and a Sunday school in progress in Manila (bottom right).

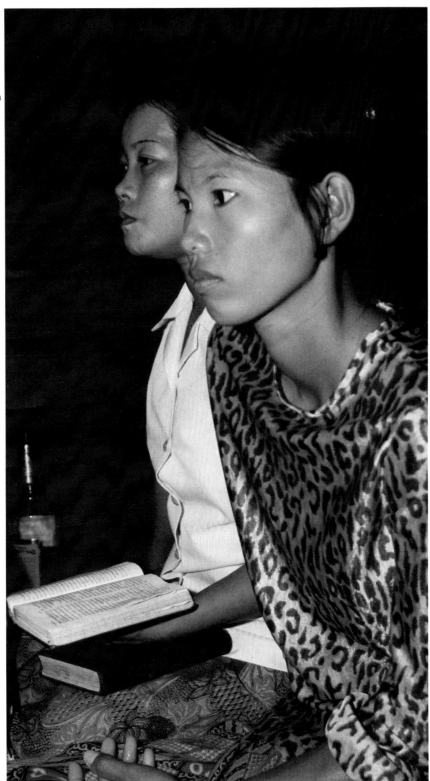

House-group at Manorom, Thailand (right).

Church members come away
from a service in Korea (above).

Different styles of church architecture: in the Yap area of Northern Thailand (left); in the traditional style of Sumatra (above); and, more unconventionally (right), a disused boat used by a church in the refugee area of Phnom Penh.

Two Christian married women from the Meo area of North Thailand attend a leadership course.

villages in Thailand, the Philippines or Japan, or in refugee settlements almost anywhere. In the city of Phnom Penh in recent years, there was a most remarkable and rapid turning of people to the Christian faith in the midst of war and famine. It seems that the traditional religious view of suffering and of human life as an illusion did not meet their needs in times of stress, and considerable numbers were becoming Christians. Although in 1972 there were only two Christian congregations in Phnom Penh, by the time of the Khmer Rouge takeover of the city, there were twenty-seven congregations.

Suffering is one of the basic problems of Asia. All men find it difficult to understand why Jesus Christ the God-man should have been allowed to suffer. The *Manual of Forcible Conversion* of Sookagakkai in Japan raises precisely this problem of the shameful death which Jesus Christ was apparently powerless to evade. Looked at from a Chinese viewpoint, the death of Jesus by Roman execution on a cross was a most remarkable loss of face. Here was a man who had made outstanding claims: to be the Son of God, to have come down from heaven, to have shared glory with his Father before the universe was made, to have all power committed to him.

Then he was put shamefully to death.

It appeared that all his claims to power and glory were false. It was meant to appear like that, for the crucifixion was a deliberate plot to discredit him. He could have been stoned as the Israelite prophets had been, but his enemies wanted him crucified in order to rob him of all respect, to deliberately destroy his credibility. There could be no Christianity and no Christians now: Christ had been publicly shown up as a fraud and a deceiver. It was all over.

How then does it come about that there are Christians in so many Asian countries, when the founder suffered the greatest loss of face in history? If he were really discredited, how does it come about that there are three million Christians in Korea and more than twice that number in Indonesia? The answer is simple. God raised Jesus to life again.

The answer is the resurrection of Jesus. It was through a real resurrection that God the Father deliberately vindicated and reinstated Jesus. It had to be a real resurrection, not a vision or a fiction. Only a real resurrection will satisfy the historical records, and account for the remarkable survival of Christian belief after such a total loss of face by Jesus on the cross.

In the last hundred years, new Christian congregations have been started, often in the face of prejudice, opposition and persecution. We have already mentioned the churches in Korea and Indonesia. The number of Christians in Taiwan doubled between 1950 and 1960. Many tribal peoples in East Malaysia, Taiwan, Thailand and the Philippines have turned from fear of evil spirits to trust in the almighty God. One of the most remarkable features of Asian life today is that Asian congregations are themselves sending out missionaries. In Thailand, there are missionaries from Japan, Hong Kong, Korea, India and Fiji. Teams have gone from Indonesia and Sarawak to other parts of South-East Asia.

Congregation in Saba, East Malaysia.

A living faith

We see that an increasing number of Asians are beginning to see a simple, basic Bible Christianity, stripped of European and American cultural accretions, as the answer to the needs of their changing societies. They find the Christian message not an outworn and outdated superstition, but a living force able to change and transform individuals, families and societies.

How does the historical fact of the death and resurrection of Jesus Christ in Asia two thousand years ago relate to the experience of Asian people today? This is often an unconscious difficulty in our understanding of the meaning of Christian belief. It is simply that it is the function of God, the Holy Spirit, to make Jesus real to us today and to communicate the life of God into our human lives. Suppose for a moment that Jesus had remained in Palestine after his death and resurrection, so that anybody who wished to establish the truth of Christianity might do so by paying a visit to Jerusalem. We could take a charter flight to Jerusalem, much as sincere Muslims make the long pilgrimage to Mecca to see where Mohammed was buried. When we arrived there, we would find the longest queue we had ever seen in our lives, even in our own crowded cities. Moreover this queue would always be getting longer because, with the population explosion, ever-increasing numbers of young people would be joining this long line waiting for an opportunity to have an interview with Jesus Christ. We should probably have to wait for years until at last our turn came to be ushered into his presence. There would only be time for a thirty-second interview because so many other people

were waiting to talk to him. That thirty-second interview would convince us once and for all that the crucified man had indeed been raised from the dead, that it is true that Jesus is both Lord and God. Returning home after our long absence all that would remain would be the precious memory of our past pilgrimage.

But Jesus chose rather to return to heaven, saying, 'It is better for you if I go away, and then I will send the Strengthener, my Spirit, to you.'

The work of his Holy Spirit is to be with each and every Christian wherever he goes and to make the presence of Jesus real to him. So what makes us Christians is that God lives in us through his Spirit. We share the new, risen life of Jesus, the life of the new creation.

In the midst of all the other significant change in Asia, it is this personal individual change which is the most significant of all. The other changes are things that happen all around us: we may be powerless to prevent them. This change is one which we can know within ourselves, simply by asking Jesus Christ to change us. He himself has already lived the most beautiful life as a human being, and through his Spirit he is willing to reproduce this same beauty in us. In dying on the cross he overcame the power of sin and evil by his suffering, and now through his Spirit he is willing to overcome that sin and evil within our own lives.

So becoming a Christian is to invite Christ by his Spirit into our lives, asking him to help us to turn from our own self-centred, sinful existence to serve the living God in newness of life. Then we will find that he is changing us progressively into Christlikeness. Still more than this, the Holy Spirit is responsible for knitting us together with other

Christians into new communities of the new humanity. It is this which we can see happening in many diverse parts of Asia today.

I shall never forget attending a midweek meeting for prayer in Seoul, Korea, one Wednesday night and finding a congregation of two thousand assembled. I listened to those two thousand all praying simultaneously, first very quietly and then rising to a tremendous crescendo of sound and then once again becoming quiet. It was an unforgettable experience.

I remember on another occasion meeting on the northern borders of Thailand a young tribesman who had set out from Northern Burma for a month's walk in order to buy a recently completed translation of the whole Bible in his own tribal language. I realized that up in those mountainous areas of Central Asia were Christian communities who were desperately concerned to know about Jesus Christ and who had realized that the teaching of the Bible could change their own lives together.

I remember being in a university in the Philippines before the declaration of Martial Law, with red-painted slogans on the walls crying for revolution, and finding there a group of a hundred Christian students duplicating manifestos to show that the message of Jesus was a radical third way, over against exploitation on the one hand and violent revolution on the other. They were not cowering in an escapist ghetto but showing the relevance of their faith to the immediate problems of their fellow Filipinos. As one student expressed it, as a Christian, one

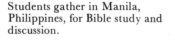

Students gather in Manila, Philippines, for Bible study and discussion.

cannot make Molotov cocktails, but at least we can make sandwiches! We hate violence but we love our fellow human beings.

Again I remember a simple gathering in a refugee tribal hut in Laos. Nearly all were illiterate, but we experienced the reality of the presence of Jesus Christ as we shared rice cakes and drank fruit juice in a simple communion service. I remember a little gathering in a bamboo leprosarium in Central Thailand. Two men with hands and feet deformed by leprosy were there for baptism, and an elder with one eye and a Bible woman with a nose eaten away by leprosy led the service. Here was another beautiful community in embryo.

Which way forward?

The photographs in this book underline the fact that we are dealing with real people in real places, who find in a changing Asia that God is real and that Jesus Christ can transform individuals through his Spirit and knit them together into new congregational communities. Does the relevance of Jesus to their world and their experience not also suggest that he might be the answer to your world and your experience?

Are we merely to be the passive, helpless victims of change? Must we just acquiesce to something which happens to us? Or, on the other hand, are we free to decide boldly to change? Are we to be pressed remorselessly into the mould of the industrialized and materialistic West, or can we decide ourselves to make a more significant change by following the Lord Jesus Christ? All the changes we described earlier in this book happen whether we want them to or not, like them or not. Conservatives and reactionaries may contrive to resist them, deplore them and long for the good old days, but change moves on remorselessly and our children inevitably will be shaped and conditioned by the changing world to which they must adapt in order to go on living.

An article in the *Singapore Mirror* quoted Arthur Koestler as saying that 'during the last explosive stages of the evolution of *Homo sapiens*, something has gone wrong; there is a flaw, some subtle engineering mistake built into our native equipment which would account for the paranoid streak running through our history . . . congenitally disordered malfunction . . . species specific disorder of behaviour'. These comments sound frighteningly true.

The same thought was expressed 1900 years earlier by a Jew named Saul (or Paul, as he was known by his Roman name) who is an early example of an Asian who received a European education. He used it to take the message of Jesus Christ from Asia into Europe. In a significant circular letter, in which he describes the new humanity and the new community, he describes the old life which this replaces as a walking death. Gautama's explanation of the world's suffering was that it was a world of illusion. Paul explains in his letter to the Ephesians, however, that man is dead in so far as any relationship or communication with his Creator is concerned: yet he continues somehow to go on walking about. Paul says that the old humanity is drifting along on the stream of this world's idea of living.

We have seen how true this is of Asia, and how we are indeed shaped and fashioned by the remorseless impersonal forces animated by the unseen evil ruler of this world. Those animistic people of the hills who still see this world populated by evil forces and spirits are perhaps not so wide of the mark. Paul goes on to suggest that we are unknowing victims of these remorseless external secular forces and of evil spiritual forces, and also that we are driven by our own inner desires. It is a frightening picture of man helpless to control his own destiny.

Do we feel that this is a true picture of Asia today, and of ourselves? This first-century writer then goes on to speak of the alienation between the Jews and the Gentile nations of the world. And still today in the twentieth century, we find that nations and races are estranged, hating and despising one another.

Such a picture of mankind would be frightening and pessimistic were it not set in a framework which shows that Jesus Christ can change all this. God is willing to make us alive through Jesus and then to remake us into a new humanity. He breaks down barriers between peoples. He overcomes the prejudices and fears between neighbours. He can bring us together into his new community.

In Sarawak, formerly part of British North Borneo, and now part of East Malaysia, there were only four thousand Lun Bawang (Murut) left. It was stated in the *Sarawak Gazette* that these people were, on average, drunk a hundred days in a year. The population of whole villages would be drunk for four or five days at a time and it was said that only the dogs were sober. In consequence of alcoholism, farming was neglected and crop production was falling. As a result of taboos and unfavourable omens, a year's crop might be abandoned and subsequently destroyed by monkeys, deer and birds, for they thought it better to starve than to offend the spirits. There was widespread malnutrition and mothers, drunk for five days in a row, neglected their children. There was a high mortality rate because of malnutrition, the children were more susceptible to disease and, because of drunkenness, they might well be neglected when they fell sick.

Here was a tribe that was killing itself off: the Rajah Brooke government finally decided to put the entire community into isolation and allow this cultural disintegration to proceed to extinction.

When these people became Christians, so many things changed. Taboos were no longer binding, alcoholism disappeared, the people became more prosperous, malnutrition was checked and the population began to increase. Meeting them today as progressive, go-ahead people whose population has practically doubled from its lowest point, one is immediately impressed by their progress. The Chinese used to say that in the old days the Chinese were way ahead of everyone, then a poor second were the Malays, the other tribes, then the dogs, and then the Muruts. The dogs would at least stay on the pavements, but the Muruts were lying in their own vomit in the gutters. Today, they say, you have the Chinese with the Muruts chasing them hard and then the Malays and then the others! Look, they say, what the Christian message has done for the Muruts.

What the Christian message has done for the Muruts it can do for other Asian communities: in fact for people throughout the world. The social evils may be more sophisticated. People's sense of need, whether it is lack of fulfilment or real misery and degradation, can be met in the same way. The same new life can be made available to all, transforming people and whole communities.

Asia is changing. Which way will it change? Do we really care? What sort of place will it be for the next generation to live in, and the next . . .? A faith that has changed some communities in Asia already can change every people and nation, if we give it the opportunity to do so.